Praise for *Agents of Healing*

Neil Miller has written an excellent and unique introduction to healing ministry. His humble and relatable approach will resonate with everyday believers who do not minister from a stage but in their day-to-day lives. His detailed examples and testimonies will encourage you, and his practical instruction will empower you to lay hands on the sick and pray for them in faith.
—Jonathan Ammon, author of *Authority Within*

In over 30 years of familiarity with various healing ministries, I have yet to find someone who operates in healing gifts who also matches Neil's ability to explain simply and encourage others to discover and develop their own God-given potential in the ministry of healing. Neil's candid stories of overcoming the fear of failure resonate to the core for anyone who desires to be used by God to see sick people become well. As Neil says, "I am writing this book for those who believe that healing still occurs today, but who don't know how to start." By the time you finish this book you will not only know how to start praying for the sick, you will never want to stop.
—Rev. Terry Bone, pastor, missionary, and author of *The Great Exchange: Passing the Baton between Generations of World Shapers*

We cannot read the Bible as a whole without seeing four verbs which encapsulate our responsibility as God's representatives on earth: preaching, teaching, praying, and healing. Most of us are comfortable with the first three; many of us don't know what to do with the fourth. But Neil does—because he has had the courage to look honestly at what the Bible says about healing and then practice it. Knowing the Scriptures and the power of God has led Neil to fruitful and Jesus-exalting ministry. I have been encouraged and inspired by his testimony as recorded in this biblically grounded book with its engaging narrative approach. Reading his book has increased my desire to grow in this most neglected aspect of our shared commission. It has also given me a path forward to being used by

God in greater measure in healing ministry—and I am confident it can do the same for you.

—Dick Brogden, co-founder of the Live Dead movement, https://www.livedead.org/

As a member of Neil's home church and a recipient of some of his prayers for healing, I found this book to be engaging and hard to put down. It was exciting to see the many positive answers to prayer as Neil simply prayed for others. It also left me with a challenge to reach out and pray for others more often. I highly recommend this book as a wonderful tool, not just for those starting out in the ministry of healing, but for all Christians as they seek to embrace their own callings to be agents of healing.

—Beth Brown, retired nursing professor, Humber College

I have personally experienced God's healing power through Neil praying for me. I often thought that the gift of healing was only for certain people. Neil's book provides a simple way to heal the sick, which Jesus demonstrated and gave us the power and authority to do. The book is easy to read, understand, and put into practice, a key principle which seemed complicated, until I read this book.

—Suresh Mather, board chair, First Alliance Church

Noah could have said, "Sometimes faith will make you look crazy until it starts to rain." This is the very nature of faith and stepping out in divine healing: hearing and obeying the father. In Agents of Healing, Neil pens a short dialogue with Jesus that marks the foundation of his work.

Jesus: Neil, are you willing to look foolish for my sake?
Me: Yes. I love you. I want to be willing to do anything for you.
Jesus: If you step out, I will be with you.
Me: Lord, this is your work. I don't know what is going to happen here. This is your church and all I am doing is what I believe you have asked me to do.

Any book by an author who has surrendered their "yes" to Jesus the way Neil has is a book I would highly recommend. Read this book and enter into the surrendered life.
—Rev. Steve Schroeder, president, Christian Ministers Association

Agents of Healing by Neil Miller is an inspiring, real-life teaching testimonial of a man's exploration into the healing ministry. With what seems like a hundred stories to illustrate every point he makes in the book, the reader is drawn along with intense interest. This is an honest book of successes and failures, and lessons learned along the way. It will ring true to your experience with healing prayer and inspire you onward toward ever-increasing success.
—Dr. Mark Virkler, founder of Communion with God Ministries, president of Christian Leadership University, and author of *4 Keys to Hearing God's Voice*

Agents of Healing promises to be a thought-provoking read, prompting deep reflection on Jesus' healing ministry during his time on earth. It will breathe new life into your healing prayers by offering a deeper understanding of how healing functions in God's kingdom. Neil's compelling stories and examples will engage you, inspiring you to take more courageous steps in your faith. This book will help you uncover and correct misconceptions about healing, empowering you to become a powerful agent of healing for God.
—Tricia Warren, pastor of Catch the Fire Okanagan, and author of *The Real Me* seminar

Also by Neil Miller

What if Listening to God Was Easy?

Agents of Healing

Learning To Do What Jesus Did

Neil Miller

Swordfish Publishing

Copyright © 2024 by Neil Miller

All rights reserved.

No part of this publication may be reproduced, stored in a retrieval system, or transmitted, in any form or in any means—by electronic, mechanical, photocopying, recording or otherwise—without prior written permission, except as permitted by Canadian copyright law.

For permission requests, contact the publisher at:

Swordfish Publishing
1 Concorde Gate, Suite 702
North York, Ontario M3C 3N6
Canada
Email: permissions@swordfish-publishing.com

ISBN 978-1-7383756-0-8 (paperback)
ISBN 978-1-7383756-1-5 (ebook)

This book is the work of the author alone. No artificial intelligence was used in the creation of the content of this book. Any use of this book for generative artificial intelligence is expressly prohibited.

This publication is designed to provide accurate and authoritative information in regard to the subject matter covered. It is sold with the understanding that neither the author nor the publisher is engaged in rendering medical advice.

Unless otherwise noted, all Scripture taken from the THE HOLY BIBLE, NEW INTERNATIONAL VERSION®, NIV® Copyright © 1973, 1978, 1984, 2011 by Biblica, Inc.® Used by permission. All rights reserved worldwide.

Scriptures marked KJV are taken from The Authorized (King James) Version. Public Domain except in the UK.

Editing by Jessica Snell Book Services, jessicasnelledits@gmail.com
Cover design by 100 Covers

For Dad and Freda
Thanks for letting me practice on you

Contents

Foreword	1
1. What on Earth Am I Doing Here?	3
2. Practice, Practice, Practice	13
3. Spiritual Gift or Spiritual Discipline?	25
4. If It Be Thy Will	37
5. Doesn't God Have a Purpose in My Sickness?	51
6. Once Upon a Time, There Was a Great King	65
7. The Fearless Policeman	77
8. Spiritual Dynamite	91
9. But I Have No Faith	107
10. The Demonic Aspect of Sickness	121
11. Training Wheels for Those Stepping Out in Healing	133
12. What About All Those Who Are Not Healed?	143
13. Why Doesn't It Always Work?	155
Conclusion: Every Prayer Counts	165
Acknowledgments	175
Bibliography	177

Foreword

Both Instant and Progressive

Knowing God is different from knowing about God. We can know about him without experiencing him. I've read about the people he healed in the Bible but I've also experienced the healing of my infirmities.

I have a long list of healings. I could write my own book about healing, but reading Neil's book is enough. This is a biblically informative and instructive treatise. Neil's many illustrations are inspiring. I am honoured that he requested me to write the foreword. I would like to share just two of my many healings.

During the first quarter of 2002, at the height of my travel as an international worker for our organization, I developed severe pain. Doctors discovered that I had liver cirrhosis and needed a transplant. But they couldn't find a donor. In addition, as a diabetic, I couldn't have the transplant if my blood sugar was not controlled. I was told I had about five years to live.

I was discouraged but I believed in the power of God to heal. Many people around the world prayed for me. In one mission gathering in Singapore, the delegates laid their hands on me and prayed for me before we received the Lord's Supper. They specifically asked God to heal and extend my life.

Last month, 22 years after the cirrhosis was discovered, the same specialist who has been taking care of me since 2002 was amazed. He had no words to explain why my liver was still functioning even after the brain hemorrhage that almost killed me, and the blood clots and diabetic problems that I've suffered. I testified to him about God's healing, and he attentively listened for the first time in two decades. Whether the healing is instant or progressive, every day I give thanks for extended life.

In July 2018, I was invited to present an academic paper at the Asian Society of Missiology in Bali, Indonesia. While I was presenting the paper to the distinguished missiologists, I developed severe abdominal pain. I was rushed to a hospital where the doctors found that I had a life-threatening condition due to three blood clots.

I was told that I must have an operation within twenty-four hours. I refused to do so without my wife present. While my wife and my nephew from Manila, a surgeon, traveled to Bali, a global prayer network interceded and prayed for my immediate healing. The president and vice-president of the Asian Society of Missiology visited me in the hospital and prayed for me. My wife and nephew arrived and negotiated with the hospital to discharge me. By faith, we traveled back to Canada, trusting the Lord for his intervention. During our six-hour stopover in Manila, we got another MRI. It showed that two of the blood clots were gone and the third one had shrunk.

God answered prayers and proved that he still heals today. Miracles still occur and prayers are powerful. Doctors and health teams are not the only agents of healing. The global church, the local church, and coworkers in the ministry who pray are all agents of healing.

Finally, we take comfort in God's promises: "For I am the LORD, who heals you" (Exodus 15:26) and "I will take away sickness from among you" (Exodus 23:25). To encourage agents of healing, I leave you with Mark 16:18: "...they will place their hands on sick people, and they will get well."

Sadiri Joy Tira, D.Min., D.Miss.
Diaspora Missiology Specialist
Jaffray Centre for Global Initiatives
at Ambrose University

Edmonton, Alberta
May, 2024

Chapter One

What on Earth Am I Doing Here?

An Introduction to Our Journey

Children's Garden School

I sat with my bent knees knocking against the kindergarten table in front of me. I could hardly imagine being in a more ridiculous situation. *What on earth am I doing here?* I had been invited to speak to a little congregation that met in a school, and I was going to talk about healing the sick in Jesus' name. Not only was I going to talk about healing, I was going to do a demonstration of actually trying to heal someone in front of the whole congregation. Who did I think I was?

It was Friday, the day when Muslims go to the mosque and many Christians in Bangladesh go to church. This tiny Baptist church met in one room of the Children's Garden School, a typical school in the overcrowded city of Dhaka. Most of the twenty or so other adults present were sitting on tiny chairs with their knees bumping into the kindergarten desks in front of them. The fact that

I, a foreigner, was the guest speaker wasn't too far out of the ordinary, but the fact that I was going to talk about healing and do a demonstration was.

A week earlier I had seen my first deliverance from an evil spirit. This was not the ordinary kind of deliverance where the recipient of prayer ministry reports feeling peaceful after being prayed for. This was the thrashing-around-on-the-floor kind and involved four adults restraining a teenage girl to prevent her from hurting herself or others.

Now it was the weekly service in the kindergarten classroom of the Children's Garden School and I was a little nervous. Sitting with my back against one of the walls, I watched as the latecomers straggled in. After a few songs and announcements, I was invited to speak. I gave my message, which recounted half a dozen testimonies of people I had prayed for, followed by a brief look at some passages in the Gospels where Jesus told his disciples to heal the sick.

Then, as my mentor had encouraged me to do, I began the demonstration. I asked anyone who had pain in their body to raise their hand. Several raised their hands. I randomly chose one woman. She seemed a bit older than some of the others in the congregation and was nicely dressed. I called her up to the front and asked about her problem. She said that she'd had pain in her knee for three months, and that the knee was hurting just then. As I began to pray aloud, I also prayed silently, *Lord, this is your work. I don't know what is going to happen here. I don't know if I am going to end up looking like a fool. This is your church and all I am doing is what I believe you have asked me to do.* I prayed for her knee and then asked her how she felt. The pain had left. She said the pain was completely gone. As she went back to her seat, I heard her telling her friends that this was for real.

My plan was for the church members to learn how to pray for each other. I asked others who had pain to stand, and I told those around them to put their hands on the sick people and rebuke the illnesses. A man named Sarkar stood up. He had back pain. A woman also stood up. They were prayed for by those around them, but experienced little or no improvement in their symptoms. I told those praying to pray again, but still there was no change.

This wasn't part of my plan.

I went over to Sarkar and put my hand on his lower back and prayed. I rebuked the spirit of pain and spoke healing into the nerves. The pain went away.

Then I went over to where the woman was standing. She told me she'd had serious lower back pain for ten years. She couldn't get up from a squatting position without holding on to the wall for support. After several prayers, this woman was also healed. She demonstrated her healing by squatting and standing up unaided.

I was blown away by everything that had happened so far. I could have prayed for several more people in that service. But seeing three people healed in less than an hour was almost too much for me. I just wanted to end the service and get out of there as quickly as possible so I could process what had just happened.

And, to be completely truthful, I was too scared of failure to continue. I wanted to leave before I prayed for someone publicly and they were not healed.

Now, looking back, I regret that I didn't pray for more people. There was much I didn't understand about healing, about persistence in prayer, and about God's perspective on our successes and failures. There was also much I didn't understand about teaching others to move in healing. A twenty-minute message was not sufficient to convince this little group that they too could do the things Jesus commanded his disciples to do. It was not sufficient to overcome the strongly held belief that only specially gifted people could heal the sick. And it was not sufficient to explain everything I had learned in the previous six months.

This book is an attempt to put my learning down in written form and encourage ordinary Christians that they can heal the sick in Jesus' name.

The Premise of This Book

In the Christian church today, there are different views on healing and usually these views are strongly held. If you are anything like me, you hold certain theological perspectives on healing, not because you have carefully studied the matter and come to your own conclusions, but because your family, your church, and people who are close to you hold the same perspectives.

In this book you are almost guaranteed to encounter ideas that contradict what you have been taught. If you find yourself reacting negatively to some things I say, could I encourage you to keep reading? Rather than putting this book down, wait to see if I can produce biblical evidence to support what I am saying. My own perspective on healing has changed over the years. I invite you to reflect on the stories and teaching in this book and ask the Lord if he has anything to teach you through them.

Now, here's my premise: Any normal, spiritually healthy Christian can learn to heal the sick in Jesus' name. Think of learning to ride a bike: any reasonably healthy, able-bodied person can do it. But just like learning to ride a bicycle, learning to heal takes some effort and investment of time. There is a price to pay in terms of being willing to look foolish, and in terms of persisting when first attempts fail. But it is possible, and it is not hard.

In this book you will see that *you can learn to heal the sick*. Let's look at that sentence more carefully.

- *<u>You</u> can learn to heal the sick*. Healing the sick is not just for spiritual superheroes. It is for ordinary disciples of Jesus like you and me.

- *You can <u>learn</u> to heal the sick*. Healing the sick was part of Jesus' discipleship curriculum that he used with the original twelve. It is still part of his discipleship curriculum today. Some learning is required, just like learning is required for any other spiritual practice.

- *You can learn to <u>heal</u> the sick*. I will demonstrate from the Bible that although the power is God's and this power is accessed through the name of Jesus when you are acting in accordance with God's will, you are the one who heals.

Why Write This Book?

In this book I will show that healing is open to all. I don't want this truth to remain hidden. More importantly, healing leads to deeper discipleship. There are many Christians for whom Christianity has become a set of truths they believe in their heads. For them, Christianity is devoid of excitement. The awareness of God's presence with them is absent. When you pray for someone and see a healing take place before your eyes, your spiritual life takes on a new and deeper dimension.

I am also writing this book for those who believe that healing still occurs today, but who don't know how to start. This book will teach and activate you.

New Learners Can Be Great Teachers

My parents, John and Helen, worked in Somalia in the 1960s. They became fluent in the Somali language, and at different times both taught in the Somali language school for foreigners. One might think, *Isn't it ridiculous to have a second-language learner be a language teacher? Surely, a native speaker would be a better choice.* But there are good reasons for involving second-language learners in the language-teaching process.

People can't always explain the grammar of the language they've grown up speaking. They may know that a particular sentence structure is incorrect, but they cannot explain *why* it is incorrect. Someone who has learned the language as an adult is in a good place to teach others because they know where new learners stumble. They can explain the material in concepts that new learners can grasp. They have lived in the new learners' shoes and understand their questions.

Many years after my parents worked in Somalia, I was in Bangladesh studying Bengali. In one class I struggled because our Bangladeshi language teacher simply could not answer our questions. He hadn't been in our shoes and couldn't understand our difficulties.

Most books on healing are written by those with decades of experience. These gifted men and women now lead large ministries and have forgotten what it's like to be a beginner. They don't remember what it is like to start from zero—to pray and not see results, to make mistakes, to feel the red-faced embarrassment of praying and seeing no change. This book is different.

I am not a native speaker of the language of healing. I was not brought up in a charismatic environment, and in Bible college I was taught a version of cessationism—that the so-called sign gifts (1 Corinthians 12:7-10) are no longer available to the church today. This book is written through the eyes of a learner. I don't claim to have all the answers. I am still learning about healing. But if you have ever prayed and not seen an answer, then I have been in your shoes and I want to share what I have learned. I fully believe that you can do everything I have done, and more.

A Note on the Stories

This book is full of stories. I am convinced that we learn best from stories. Although in many cases names and minor details have been changed to protect privacy, unless noted in the text, none of the stories are fictionalized accounts or composites of several people.

Where do the stories come from? In December 2019 I started maintaining a prayer and healing record. I tried to list everyone I prayed for, what their problems were, how I prayed, and what the results were. When possible, I typed up the notes the day I prayed. In many cases, I have been able to go back to the people whose stories are used in this book, check my write-up for accuracy, and get their permission to include their story. The majority of those contacted were happy for me to use their real names in this book, and I have honored their desire. Most of the stories took place either in Ontario or in Bangladesh, the two places I lived during the writing process.

An Overview of Where We Are Going

Some people like to have a bird's-eye view of the journey before they set out. For those who like to have a map, here is where we are going:

- Chapter 2: Practice, Practice, Practice. In this chapter, you will learn one key ingredient that will enable you to shift from being someone who prays and rarely sees results to someone who prays and frequently sees results.

- Chapter 3: Spiritual Gift or Spiritual Discipline? In this chapter you will discover from the Bible that healing others is open to all, regardless of whether or not you have the spiritual gift of healing.

- Chapter 4: If It Be Thy Will. In this chapter you will see why it is incorrect to apply the biblical accounts of Paul's thorn and Job's troubles to your sickness.

- Chapter 5: Doesn't God Have a Purpose in My Sickness? In this chapter you will learn that it is usually a waste of time to look for a beneficial purpose in bad events that befall you. You will also explore the relationship between sin and sickness.

- Chapter 6: Once Upon a Time, There Was a Great King. This chapter explains the role of your agency and initiative in healing.

- Chapter 7: The Fearless Policeman. In this chapter you will take an in-depth look at your spiritual authority and how to use it.

- Chapter 8: Spiritual Dynamite. Here you will discover surprising yet biblical teaching about power.

- Chapter 9: But I Have No Faith. Most people wrongly understand faith as working themselves up to believe something. This chapter explains what faith is and how to develop it.

- Chapter 10: The Demonic Aspect of Sickness. Demons are real and sometimes they make you sick.

- Chapter 11: Training Wheels for Those Stepping Out in Healing. When you are learning something new, it is helpful to have a step-by-step procedure. After you become skilled, you can discard the training wheels.

- Chapter 12: What About All Those Who Are Not Healed? Honest people involved in healing ministry readily admit that not everyone is healed. This chapter shows you how to handle a failed healing in a way that is both loving toward the one prayed for and gentle on yourself.

- Chapter 13: Why Doesn't It Always Work? Continuing from the previous chapter, this chapter explores some reasons why people are not healed.

- Conclusion: Every Prayer Counts. Your prayers have impact even when you don't initially see any results.

Each chapter opens with a story. Each chapter tackles a wrong belief and replaces it with biblical truth. Each chapter ends with a prayer.

Elim Lodge

My wife, Ingrid, and I were spending a week at Elim Lodge, a Christian campground and summer trailer park beside a beautiful lake in Ontario. We were the international workers in residence and were tasked with giving a ten-minute report mornings and evenings during the week. This was followed by Bible teaching by another speaker. My ten-minute talks had gone well. I simply reported on people who had encountered Jesus during our previous term in Bangladesh.

While I was out jogging one afternoon, prior to the talk that evening, God spoke to me,[1] saying, *Make it real for the people in the audience.* For me, making it real meant inviting anyone in the audience who wanted prayer for physical healing to come forward, and I would pray for that person in front of the whole

---

1. In this book, when I say, "God spoke to me," I am referring to thoughts and impressions that come from the Holy Spirit. For more on this subject, please refer to Mark Virkler's excellent teaching segment found at www.CWGministries.org/4keys or my previous book, *What if Listening to God Was Easy?*

group. This campground is owned and operated by a Christian organization and, like many evangelical churches, praying and expecting immediate healing is not the normal practice there. My immediate—clearly faith-filled—response was *No way. God, I need a sign before I do something like that.* My dialogue with the Lord continued as follows:

Jesus: Neil, are you willing to look foolish for my sake?
Me: Yes. I love you. I want to be willing to do anything for you.
Jesus: If you step out, I will be with you.
Me: Ok, I give up my request for a sign, but please help me. This is scary.

That evening I prefaced my talk by saying that I was going to continue my previous theme, but if anyone wanted prayer, I would pray for them at the end of my talk. One woman's hand shot up before I had finished my sentence. I finished my talk and invited her forward. I gave her a chair to sit on facing the audience and pulled up a chair beside her. Her husband came up with her and sat in the front row.

I asked what her prayer need was. She told us that she had been having inflammation all over her body and pain in her heart. At that moment she assessed her heart pain to be five out of ten, with ten being the worst. The doctors had checked it out, but had not found anything wrong with her heart. She had been suffering in this way for eight months.

I invited the audience to join me in prayer. I emphasized that they could all do what I did, that I was not special, and that praying for the sick was for all believers. I put my hand on her shoulder and started praying. I began by praising God for his power and authority over all the powers of darkness. I hadn't gotten very far when I remembered that I usually pray for the sick with my eyes open. I opened them and saw that she was trying to get the attention of her husband, whose head was reverently bowed. I stopped praying and asked if she had anything to share. She took the microphone and said, "The pain is gone. It left as soon as you put your hand on me."

I was grateful for this dramatic confirmation of the things I had been saying. Instantaneous healing still occurs today. You can learn to heal the sick, just as I learned to heal the sick.

Closing Prayer

You can learn to heal the sick in Jesus' name. That is what this book is about. In the next chapter I'll share more of my story, but before we go there, why don't you take a moment to pray?

Lord, I've heard testimonies about healing. I've read about healing in the Bible. But I want to experience this in my own life. I don't want a form of Christianity that is limited to precepts I believe in my head. I want your life to flow through me and touch those whom I interact with who need your touch. One more thing, Father. As I read this book, help me to stay fully within the bounds of your written Word, the Bible. I pray this in Jesus' name.

Chapter Two

Practice, Practice, Practice

Focused Practice Is Key to Growing in Healing

Wrong belief: When the power of God is involved, no practice is necessary.

Biblical truth: We must learn and practice if we want to consistently heal the sick.

The Guard

Just like millions of others crowded into the megacity of Dhaka, we lived in a multistory apartment building. The ground level had parking space for the tenants who owned cars and a cooking area and bedroom where the three guards slept when they weren't on duty. During the day, the guards and drivers hung out on the ground level. Above this level were six floors of apartments, two apartments per floor.

One day as I left our apartment to get something from a nearby shop, Jewel, one of the guards, greeted me in the deep voice of one whose cold had descended into his chest. I wondered if I should offer to pray for him. Not feeling confident, I kept walking. On the way to the shop, I set three conditions before the Lord. *Lord, if he is still present when I get back, if he is alone, and if he is willing to come up to our apartment, then I will pray for him.*

I returned from the shop a few minutes later. Jewel was still on duty, and no one was talking to him. I asked if he would like me to pray for him. He agreed. I asked if he would come up to my apartment. He agreed. He called another guard to watch the gate while he came upstairs with me.

After seating him on our couch, I explained to Jewel, a Muslim, that I wanted to pray for him in Jesus' name. Again, he agreed. I cupped my hands together and lifted them to chest height as Muslims do when they pray. I rebuked the sickness in Jesus' name and prayed for Jewel's healing. Then the prayer was over, and he got up and left. I thought, *Well, Lord, I am pretty sure I did what you wanted me to do. The results are in your hands.* Not five minutes later, the intercom rang. I picked it up and Jewel exclaimed, "Sir, sir, the fever is gone!"

Successes and Failures

Many years earlier, I lived in a town in western Bangladesh. One day on the street, I ran into one of my friends, Shetu. Trying to practice local politeness, I asked him how he was, how his wife was, and how his family was. He told me that his mother was sick with asthma. In a fit of courage, I offered to go to their house and pray for her. When I got to their house, she was sitting in a chair hyperventilating. I prayed for her as best I knew how. Shortly after my prayer was over, her breathing became normal. I, being quite shy and introverted, didn't know how to take advantage of this opportunity to share anything about Jesus. I just got up and left.

But not all my experiences were positive. The first time I ever laid my hands on someone to pray for them was in Khartoum, Sudan. At the time, I was teaching at a small Bible college for displaced Christians from southern Sudan. The child of one of my students was sick. Eager to learn how to pray for people but not bold enough to do it on my own, I convinced a colleague to go with me to the hospital. I parked the Jeep I was borrowing at the hospital entrance and found the parents with their newborn baby. The baby had diarrhea and was suffering from dehydration. I laid hands on the baby and prayed. Five minutes later, the baby died.

Another time, I was attending a birthday party for a girl who lived in our building in Dhaka. In Bangladesh, childhood birthday parties are more for the benefit of the parents than the children. The parents invited their wealthy and connected friends to an upscale restaurant. Everyone dressed to impress. My wife, Ingrid, ended up sitting next to a well-known national television personality. I sat next to a retired government official who had held a senior position in the Department of Fisheries. As I talked with the official, I learned that he had pain in his knee. I told him that I would be happy to pray for him, though the noisy restaurant environment was not that conducive to prayer. He agreed to come to my home a few days later.

When he came, I seated him in my living room and, after a bit of conversation, tried every prayer I had in my repertoire. Not one of them worked. After half an hour of trying, he left in exactly the same condition he had entered. Needless to say, I was more than a little embarrassed.

Lord, I Need Someone to Teach Me

Clearly, I needed some help. I had come to the conclusion that discipleship is not just believing what Jesus taught, but doing what Jesus did—including healing people.[1] I was convinced that healing was in the Bible and was for today, but my own history of praying for people was checkered with more failures than successes. I needed a teacher.

---

1. If you are looking for biblical support for this claim, hang on, it's coming. Wait until the next chapter.

Sitting in the living room praying one evening in April 2019, I explained to the Lord that it wasn't fair. "Your disciples had you as a teacher," I said. "I have no one to teach me how to heal."

The Lord reminded me that almost every time we had someone over for a meal, I thought that I should offer to pray for them. Usually, I was too self-conscious to do so. The Lord showed me that he had given me opportunities to practice, but most of the time I was too scared to step out and pray. Having a teacher wouldn't do much good if I wasn't going to actually pray for people. If I was going to learn, I would need to practice, and practice a lot.

During this stage of my journey, I didn't have a true understanding of God's love for me, and so I would frequently get caught up in a cycle of guilt. I would meet someone who had a need, but wouldn't pray. After they left, I would view the situation as a missed opportunity. Then I would feel guilty and upset at myself for letting the Lord down. Then I would beat myself up for a while and resolve to try to do better next time.

I knew that this cycle of missed opportunity, followed by guilt, followed by putting pressure on myself was not helpful. So I told the Lord, "I can't handle waiting for random opportunities to pray for people. If you are going to teach me how to heal, then I need regular opportunities to pray." Then I put a special request to the Lord: "Give me three opportunities to pray for the sick each week." In the months that followed, every week when I prayed this prayer faithfully, I got three opportunities to pray for the sick. Perhaps the opportunities to pray were always there but I just hadn't noticed them before. Or perhaps the Lord gave me special opportunities. Often, they were little things. Someone had a headache in the office. Another had a cold at church. Someone's back hurt. The opportunities were there, and I started to take them. Sometimes I even got three opportunities in a single day.

Those receiving the prayers were happy to be prayed for. Offering to pray for someone on the spot was invariably received as an expression of love and compassion. But hardly anyone reported instantaneous healing. Often, my wife reports, I would come home from my office frustrated because I prayed for someone yet again, and they were not healed.

After about six months of praying and not seeing many results, I met Michael, a visitor to Bangladesh. When I found out that Michael frequently prayed for people and saw healings, I asked him to coach me. Michael played an instrumental role in helping me step out in healing. He taught me to ask what the level of pain was before and after I prayed. He helped me interpret some phenomena I didn't understand. He encouraged me to keep going when I was discouraged. He taught me the importance of command in healing. (We'll look at some of these ideas in more detail in later chapters.) Michael also encouraged me to be bold and do things I would never have had the courage to do on my own—like the healing demonstration described in the previous chapter. In addition, Michael loved me and prayed for me. Shortly after this, I began to see instantaneous healings.

Encouraging Results

In October of that year, I prayed for Jasmine. She had had a cough for several months and it just wouldn't go away. When I prayed for her, she felt lightheaded and wanted to sit down. At first, I thought, *Oh no. I prayed for her and she got worse.* I learned later that this sense of being lightheaded was how she perceived the Holy Spirit's touch. She told me that she felt a cool wind in her chest when I prayed for her. The cough was gone within a few days.

In November, Payel, in whose apartment the house church met, was too sick to attend church. After the service was over, I asked her husband if I could pray for her. He went into her bedroom to check, and then told me to come into their room. I found her lying on the bed, feeling too sick to even sit up. I put my hand on her head and prayed for her. After my first prayer, her headache went away. I prayed again and her blocked nose cleared up. Then she felt well enough to sit up. As she sat on the edge of her bed, she complained of terrible throat pain. I thought about putting my hand on her throat, but that seemed to be breaking too many social norms in a culture where men and women do not even shake hands. I prayed for her throat, but there was no change. Still, I was pleased with a two-out-of-three success rate.

About a week later, Hemel and his wife came to our home for a visit. Hemel had struggled with asthma since childhood. After climbing the four flights of stairs to our apartment, he would often need to settle down for a bit before his breathing returned to normal. That day, three of us prayed for Hemel: Ingrid, Shewly (his wife), and me. After the prayer, he told us that he felt good. The next day from his office he messaged me to say that he still felt good. The following weekend he gave testimony in his church that he had been healed.

About a week later, at the house church, Ferdaus Chanchal had a bad head cold. His nose had been constantly dripping that morning. Before praying for him, I asked him what the severity of his cold was on a scale of one to ten, with ten being the worst. He said it was five out of ten. I put my hand on his shoulder and prayed. Then I asked him what the severity was. He waited a while and then said, "One out of ten." Then he waited a while longer and said, "It's gone." He had been waiting to see if his nose would keep dripping. When he was sure that it had stopped, he declared his cold to be gone. Prakash, another member of the church, was sitting beside me, observing what was happening. Two weeks later Prakash was sick. I prayed for him, and he immediately felt better.

I continued to practice praying for people and the healings continued to occur. In December, I went to visit a Muslim friend named Shofique. When I got to his house, I saw that he had a special back support cushion on his chair to relieve his back pain. I asked if he would like prayer. He agreed. I prayed for him, and the pain went away immediately.

Trying This at a Conference

I was excited over the healings I had been seeing and yet longed to see more. I wanted to keep practicing and so I took all the opportunities I could find to pray for people. Since I was just learning, I didn't have a reputation to uphold or much fear about what would happen if the person I prayed for was not healed. I was happy to pray for anyone I could find. More opportunities to practice were soon to come.

Winter in Bangladesh is the season for conferences. The fields are bare, and the weather is no longer stifling hot. Our organization had its family conference in January. I told the organizers that I would be happy to pray for anyone who was sick during the conference. The organizers announced this from the podium and made a room available for this purpose. Not everyone who came for prayer experienced instantaneous healing, but many did.

Hazera came complaining of weakness in her right hand and pain in her neck. She couldn't lift her right arm above shoulder height. I suspected a pinched nerve. Ingrid, my wife, is a physiotherapist, and I thought this was a problem that a good physiotherapist could treat quite effectively. But Ingrid wasn't around, and Hazera had come to me for prayer, so I did what I knew to do. I rebuked the pain in Jesus' name and then asked her to move her arm around to check it out. She did. The pain was gone.

Nafisa told me that she had had back pain for a year. I prayed a simple prayer of rebuke, and she was healed. I told her to twist back and forth to check it out. Her face registered her surprise at being healed just like that. I told her to rebuke the pain herself if it came back.

Shewly came to see me during the morning tea break. She looked terrible and could barely talk above a whisper. She also had pain in her neck and shoulder and could hardly move her head. I took her into the vacant dining area since the room where we usually prayed was occupied. I was in a bit of a hurry because I thought it was time for the meeting to start. I prayed for her, rebuking the sickness. Her body jerked when I prayed. I had her move around to check out how she was feeling. She reported that her neck and shoulder were better. Then she wanted me to pray for the pain in her throat. I did. It also immediately improved. She could now talk almost normally. She still had some pain in her throat, but she believed she would recover without further prayer.

This all seemed too easy, and I wondered if what I was seeing was real. Six weeks later I saw Hazera at another meeting. I asked her how she was. She said that the pain never came back, and she swung her arm around like a windmill to show me that all was well. Ingrid, who was with me this time, commented in understated physiospeak, "It looks like she has full range of motion." I saw

Nafisa more than two and a half months later. She said that she was not bothered by the back pain I had prayed for.

I ended up praying individually for twenty-one people at this conference. Six experienced immediate healing. Several others experienced God's touch in some way. Not everyone was healed, but what I was seeing now was a whole lot more than what I had been seeing in the past. Some nights I was so excited over the visible demonstration of God's power that it was hard to fall asleep.

About two weeks later, I was teaching in Gazipur. There, a Muslim woman who cooked at the facility where I was staying came to see me. She had heard that I prayed for people at the family conference and so she plucked up the courage to ask for prayer. She'd had pain in her right elbow for several months. I prayed for her. After prayer, as was now my practice, I asked if there was any change. We had been speaking Bengali and she responded with a one-word answer: "None." She kept repeating the word: "None. None. None."

Getting a negative response to my question was disappointing, but I mentally prepared myself to pray for her again. It took me several seconds to figure out that she wasn't saying "none" meaning "there is no change." Instead, she meant "there is no pain." The look on her face betrayed her surprise at what she was experiencing. She continued bending and straightening her elbow, repeating, "There is no pain."

Leg Acne

At times, God used me despite my ignorance. Three days after praying for the Muslim woman, I attended a conference for youth and young adults. There Aminul told me his story. He had run away from home to Dhaka because his parents wanted him to quit his studies in order to work to support the family. He came to faith in Christ while away from home and was baptized a few years later.

However, Aminul had some health problems. He woke up nightly feeling feverish, he had a mouth sore, and he had some strange form of acne on his thighs. Aminul also told me that he had been in a relationship with a girl and had made a proposal of marriage. The mother agreed to the marriage, but the father did not. Three months later, the girl committed suicide in protest of her father's refusal. Aminul was feeling troubled and depressed.

I thought I would deal with Aminul's grief before praying for his health problems. I put my hand on his shoulder and prayed and rebuked evil spirits, particularly those that might have attached themselves to his grief. After the prayer, he said, "My mind feels free. I no longer feel sad or weighed down. I feel relieved."[2] Then he felt something on his legs; there was some kind of sensation where the acne was. The itching stopped. He went away to check. The acne looked the same, but still he felt different. He returned to his chair, and I kept my hand hovering near his shoulder. My hand got warm. He sat for a long time. He told me that he felt good.

The next morning Aminul came to give me an update. For the first time in a long time, he had not had a fever at night. There were no new acne spots on his legs, and he believed the existing ones would go away. During the night, he had a dream where he saw something leave his chest. This, I believe, was a pictorial representation of the demonic oppression that he had been experiencing. He was happy and I was filled with joy to the point of tears. He messaged me more than two years later and told me that he was doing well.

The Importance of Practice

Malcolm Gladwell, quoting studies by Daniel Levitin, has popularized the ten-thousand-hour rule.

> The emerging picture from such studies is that ten thousand hours of practice is required to achieve the level of mastery

---

2. Dealing with grief by rebuking evil spirits is a very simplistic approach to a complex emotional problem. If I were to meet someone like Aminul now, I would adopt an inner healing approach to ministry. At the time, I used the tools I had available to me, and God worked through me despite my inexperience.

associated with being a world-class expert—in anything....No one has yet found a case in which true world-class expertise was accomplished in less time.[3]

If you give ten thousand hours of focused attention to anything, you will achieve a high level of proficiency.[4] Focused practice breeds expertise. We intuitively understand this in the natural realm. But when it comes to the spiritual realm, we think a person ought to be able to operate without practice.[5] That is simply not true. Praying for the sick requires practice.

Conclusion

If you are going to be used by God to bring healing to others, you must practice praying for the sick. And, in my case at least, practice a lot. I went through a period of six months of learning where I saw more failures than successes. Your journey may not be the same as mine, but one thing is certain: if you want to heal the sick, learning and practice are required. Unless you are a person of unusually high drive and fortitude, you will also need teachers, coaches, and mentors along the way.

---

3. Gladwell, *Outliers*, 29.

4. If you do an Internet search on the ten-thousand-hour rule, you will find some detractors. For example, several have clarified that ten thousand hours is not an exact number and that the practice must be deliberate. No one, however, disputes Gladwell's core idea: lots of practice is required for elite performance. Even if a person does not achieve world-class expertise, they will improve with deliberate practice. For several clarifications to Gladwell's rule, see David Bradley's "Why Gladwell's 10,000-hour Rule Is Wrong."

5. For a detailed study of the importance of practice in the whole of one's spiritual life, see Dallas Willard's *The Spirit of the Disciplines*.

Key Bible Passages

There are several passages in the Bible that address this aspect of spiritual training. And we know that good training almost always includes a lot of practice. Here are two passages that emphasize training:

> The student is not above the teacher, but everyone who is fully trained will be like their teacher. (Luke 6:40)

> Everyone who competes in the games goes into strict training. They do it to get a crown that will not last, but we do it to get a crown that will last forever. (1 Corinthians 9:25)

Teaser

In the next chapter we will see from the Bible that healing was never intended to be limited to the special few. Ministering healing is something that Jesus intended for every one of his disciples.

Closing Prayer

Lord Jesus, sometimes I want to see results but I don't always like the discipline that is required to see those results. Help me to be willing to practice praying for people with as much dedication as athletes practice sports. Help me to accept your training regimen, even when it is hard.

Chapter Three

Spiritual Gift or Spiritual Discipline?

Healing Is Part of the Discipleship Journey

> *Wrong belief: Healing people in Jesus' name is limited to the special few.*
>
> *Biblical truth: Healing is part of the ordinary Christian's walk of discipleship.*

Neil, We Think You Have a Gift

It was now five months after I had started seeing healings occur more regularly and I wanted to tell others what I had been learning. One February morning, during our organization's quarterly team leaders' meeting, I told the other leaders what had been happening. I shared a few testimonies and then made my main point: they could do what I was doing if they were willing to spend the time in learning and practice. Although the other leaders rejoiced with me in the miracles that I had seen, their reaction was not quite what I expected. One of them said, "Neil, maybe you have the gift of healing." Others assented.

If healing is a special gift given only to a select few, then those without the gift would not be able to do what I had done. I didn't believe that what I was doing was inaccessible to others in the room, but I didn't know how to prove my point during the meeting that morning.

Healing and Discipleship

Is healing a special gift reserved for the chosen few? Or is healing supposed to be part of our discipleship journey? We can't go wrong if we look at what Jesus did.

As we read through the Gospels, we see Jesus' method of making disciples.[1] First, Jesus called several people to be with him, to learn from him. As they spent time with him, they saw him in action. They saw how he "healed many who had various diseases" (Mark 1:32–34). Jesus, being the greatest teacher, gave them opportunities to practice doing what he had been doing. After a while it was time for them to branch out on their own and heal people when Jesus was not with them (Mark 3:14–15; Luke 9:1–6; Matthew 10:1–8).

The journey of learning is not always filled with stories of success. There are failures too, and the disciples under Jesus' tutelage were no exception. There were times when they could not heal (Matthew 17:14–16). When they failed, Jesus explained to them the reason behind their failure (vv. 19–20). Their failures were not only failures of faith, but there were also failures of compassion (Luke 9:12) and failures of attitude (Luke 9:54). Yet Jesus continued to instruct.

Despite the setbacks he faced with his disciples, Jesus did not give up on his attempts to train ordinary people to do the things he was doing. After sending out the twelve disciples to preach and heal (Luke 9:1–2), Jesus broadened out and sent seventy-two others who were not in his inner circle of disciples to do the same thing (Luke 10:1–9). The seventy-two came back full of joy over what

---

1. The root meaning of "disciple" is "learner." *Mickelson's*, s.v. "G3101 mathetes."

had happened (v. 17). Their spiritual lives came alive. Now they were not just mentally assenting to some great teaching they had heard. They were actually doing the same things that Jesus had done. Healing was part of their discipleship journey.

Could I do what Jesus did? Could I teach people to heal?

Doing What Jesus Did

My colleagues had told me that they thought I had the gift of healing. If I could choose a handful of people and train them to heal others in Jesus' name, then the argument that what I was doing was not accessible to them because I had the gift of healing and they did not would crumble. Shortly after, I had the opportunity to try out my idea.

Foyez and Jasmine

At the end of April, I met with Foyez and Jasmine for a spiritual coaching session. I started off by having them read several passages in the Gospels where Jesus healed people. We saw how healing was mediated by command (John 4:46–54), by rebuke (Mark 1:21–28), and by touch (Mark 1:29–31). We saw that faith was important (Matthew 8:1–4 and 5–13). We also looked at how Jesus gave authority to his disciples to heal (Matthew 10:1–8) and how we have been given the same authority (Matthew 28:18–20).[2] Then I gave them homework. I told them to ask God for opportunities to pray for the sick. I told them to pray for the sick people they encountered and then tell me how it went when we met next time.

We met again two weeks later. They both had had several opportunities to pray for the sick. In most of the cases they reported, the sick person got well.

---

2. We look at the importance of command and our authority in chapter 7. We look at faith in chapter 9. And we look at Matthew 28:18–20 below.

Yet, they struggled with doubt. Was the recovery due to their prayers or was it simply the natural process of healing?

During that meeting I asked if either of them had physical issues. Foyez had a mildly sore throat. He had been worried about this for a few days, wondering if a larger problem was developing. I gave instructions to Jasmine: put your hand on his throat, invite the Holy Spirit to come, wait until you feel God's presence, then tell the sickness to go away. As she did this, Foyez felt pressure on his face. It felt to him like something went out of him. He felt good.

We met again two weeks after that. In this meeting I learned that they had been praying for the sick, but not in their presence. They would take the prayer requests home and then pray for the sick person while they were alone at home. I, however, wanted them to develop the courage to pray for the sick person right then and there. By this time COVID-19 restrictions were limiting movement, so I encouraged them to pray for the sick over the phone.

The next day, Foyez prayed for a colleague over Zoom. The colleague had had a cough for three months. Foyez first invited the Holy Spirit to come, then he commanded the sickness to leave. His colleague felt warm. A few days later when Foyez went to the office, he found that she was completely well. In just four weeks after first bringing up the subject with them, they were seeing healings.

Mofazzel

Mofazzel was another person I wanted to encourage in praying for the sick. I started off by sharing some Scripture passages with him. Then I shared how I asked the Lord for three opportunities per week to pray for the sick. Mofazzel was uncomfortable with that idea. He consented to asking the Lord for one opportunity to pray for a sick person before our next meeting two weeks later.

One day, when he was ready to try, he prayed that God would give him an opportunity to minister to a sick person. Later that day, a chance to pray for his older sister came up. For three years she had been largely bedridden and unable to put weight on her foot. Before calling his sister that evening, Mofazzel asked for a sign from the Lord. If his sister was lying on her bed when he called, but not sleeping, he would understand that God wanted to heal her. He did pray, and the wound on her foot dried up a few days later.

If there ever was a case of a disciple becoming greater than his teacher, Mofazzel is an example. By September of that year, he had become very bold and was seeing many people healed. His colleague Akir had COVID-19 symptoms and could not talk due to his difficulty breathing. After Mofazzel prayed for him, he talked for a long time. Another believer from Mofazzel's home village was sick. The villagers were sure he was going to die and were planning to create problems over his burial.[3] Their plans fell apart when he was healed in response to Mofazzel's prayer.

Xaver

It wasn't only people I was in a mentoring relationship with who learned to pray for healing. Xaver was simply a friend with whom I had talked about learning to heal. I told Xaver what I had done and encouraged him to do the same. Weeks later, Xaver shared over email how God had used him to heal someone: "Yesterday we held a parents' meeting for the participants of our Vocational Training Program. One mother complained about pain in her knees. I prayed for one of her knees. Then she told me to pray for her other knee. Then she sat and talked for a while with my staff. Later she told me that her pain has gone, and she feels much better. What a blessing!"

My own experience has demonstrated that we can train people to heal in Jesus' name.

---

3. Sometimes followers of Jesus who have not assimilated into a traditional church face problems at the time of the burial of a loved one. Christians cannot be buried in a Muslim cemetery and churches are reluctant to accept the bodies of nonmembers for burial.

The Missing Part of the Great Commission

Healing is not only part of the discipleship journey that Jesus mapped out for his followers, but it is also part of reaching out to others. We see this in the Great Commission passages of Scripture.

> Then Jesus came to them and said, "All authority in heaven and on earth has been given to me. Therefore go and make disciples of all nations, baptizing them in the name of the Father and of the Son and of the Holy Spirit, and teaching them to obey everything I have commanded you. And surely I am with you always, to the very end of the age." (Matthew 28:18–20)

Most people use this passage to urge others to go and preach the gospel. This means telling people how Jesus died on the cross for our sins and came back to life on the third day, and that through believing in him we have eternal life. Certainly this is important and these are things we ought to teach and share, but this is not all. The passage says, "teaching them to obey everything I have commanded you."

Jesus taught his disciples many things. He taught them to love their enemies. He taught them how to pray. He taught them to forgive. He taught that he was the door, the way of salvation. He also taught them to heal and to drive out demons.

We have gotten part of Jesus' teaching down pat. We can easily explain that Jesus is the way of salvation. We are happy to repeat Jesus' teaching about loving our enemies. But we have missed a core element. On Missions Sunday in church, we don't normally hear our pastor telling us to go and heal the sick, even though this is a significant part of what Jesus commanded his disciples to do. We have contented ourselves with knowing what Jesus taught, but not doing what Jesus did. We are not obeying everything Jesus commanded.

How does this work in practice? Let's look at a few examples.

A Sprained Wrist

Parvez came over to visit one Friday evening. Although he politely talked to me, what he really wanted was Ingrid's medical advice. Parvez's injury had occurred the previous week during the Muslim feast of Eid al-Adha, when faithful Muslims kill a cow or goat in memory of when Abraham went to sacrifice his son. While lifting a heavy pot of meat, Parvez had sprained his wrist. Ingrid examined the wrist and told him that he should purchase a brace to wear while the wrist healed.

Then after Ingrid left to make tea, I offered to pray for him. I put my hand on his wrist and rebuked the pain in Jesus' name. After my prayer, Parvez held his arm vertically and moved his wrist back and forth, evidently without discomfort. "Where did you learn how to do that?" he asked. I wasn't sure how to answer Parvez's question. The only thing I could think to do was to open my Bible and read a passage. I turned to Mark 11 and talked about Jesus cursing the fig tree and the importance of having faith in God. That was the first time I had ever read the Bible with Parvez.

A Painful Foot

Ingrid and I were visiting our good friends Abbas and Rabiya. Rabiya had been suffering from headaches and so we came over so that I could pray for her. After praying for her, I felt the presence of God remaining on my hands,[4] so I turned to Abbas and prayed for him. Both Abbas and Rabiya then told me that I should pray for their son, Rafik, who was still at work.

Rafik came in a bit later, limping due to a bad corn on his foot. His parents told him that I was going to pray for him. I had the Bible on my phone open to Acts 3, the passage about Peter and John healing the crippled beggar. I wanted Rafik to understand that the healing was not due to my own power or godliness (v. 12), but that the power came from faith in the name of Jesus (v. 16).

---

4. I talk about physical phenomena in chapter 8.

After Rafik read the passage, I asked what his pain level was. He replied that it was seven out of ten. I prayed for him and the pain went down to four out of ten. He was surprised. I had him walk around to check it out. He could walk better than before, but the pain was not completely gone.

In Bangladesh, except in special situations,[5] it is never appropriate to touch another person's foot. This time, with Rafik's permission, I placed my hand on his foot to pray for him. I touched the corn, but that was too painful, so I put my hand on the top of his foot and prayed.

After this prayer, he pressed on the corn himself and there was no pain unless he pushed right on the center of it. Again, he was surprised. By this point he was walking normally. He strode into the other room where his wife and Ingrid were sitting to demonstrate to her that now he could walk normally. Praying for Rafik's foot was an opportunity to give testimony about Jesus.

A Pain in the Chest

During our organization's staff family conference in 2022, we announced a time when people could come and receive prayer for physical healing. I was praying with my friend Mofazzel. Nafisa brought her husband, Khalid, for prayer. He was complaining of pain in his chest on the right side, below the rib cage. He used to drive a van rickshaw,[6] but because of the pain he had stopped two months earlier. Before I prayed, I said, "Muslims believe that Jesus was taken straight up to heaven, but we believe that Jesus died and rose again and then went to heaven." Khalid answered in no uncertain terms that Jesus didn't die. In accordance with Muslim doctrine, he told us that someone who looked like him was crucified in his stead and that Jesus himself was taken straight up to heaven.

---

5. A way to highly honor an older person is to stoop down and touch their feet. If someone accidentally touches the foot of another person, both parties immediately apologize.

6. This is a bicycle rickshaw with a flat bed, used for hauling cargo.

I said, "If we pray for you with the belief that Jesus died and rose again, and if you are healed, what impact will that have on your beliefs?" Khalid said, "Then I'll have to believe you." I prayed and the pain decreased. I prayed again and the pain decreased yet again but was still there just a little. Mofazzel prayed just once, and the pain left completely. Khalid went away with a thoughtful look on his face.

What about the Spiritual Gift of Healing?

If healing others is supposed to be part of our walk of discipleship, then where does the gift of healing fit in? In 1 Corinthians 12:7–10 Paul gives a list of spiritual gifts, of which healing is one. For much of my life, my reasoning went something like the following: if only some people have the gift of healing, then others, by definition, do not have that gift. If they do not have that gift, then they cannot heal. If they can't heal, then what is the use of trying to pray for the sick? *If only I had the gift of healing,* my heart would cry out, *then I could pray for people and they would recover.*

This kind of reasoning limits us. It groups us into the spiritual haves and the have-nots. There is something radically wrong with this way of thinking. Let's find out what it is by looking at my short-lived musical career.

The Dog Wailed

I was in the eighth grade, sitting on the couch in my music teacher's house for my weekly trumpet lesson. Mr. Noden was sitting on a chair in front of me and his dog was at his feet. He raised his trumpet to his lips and sounded a clear C note. His dog lay there silently. Then Mr. Noden told me to play the same note. I tried. His dog howled. "See, you're not hitting the note. My dog can tell." He demonstrated again, and again his dog lay peacefully at his feet. I tried again, and again the dog howled. This was the start of the end of my musical career.

It had started in first grade in a private school where swimming and music lessons were part of the curriculum. Although I did improve in swimming, I did not advance much in music. My father, however, was insistent that his children receive opportunities that he never had as a farm boy in the Saskatchewan prairie. He encouraged each of his children to take music lessons. I wanted to play the guitar but was told that I should learn piano first. After struggling through several years of piano lessons, I did get to the point where I could play a few songs that could be identified as music. On my way to guitar, I got distracted by the idea of playing the trumpet. After the disastrous lessons with Mr. Noden and his dog, I quit music altogether.

Yet, twenty years later, I could still bang out a memorized song on the piano. Although I had no inherent musical ability, I could still learn to play a musical instrument.

Spiritual Training

Praying for healing is much the same, only easier. Some people are supernaturally gifted. Praying for healing comes easy to them. With just a little bit of instruction and practice, they are seeing people get healed. Others have no gifting in healing, but they can still learn how to heal people.

Did the Twelve and the seventy-two all have the spiritual gift of healing? I am certain they did not. Yet, they all learned to heal. Likewise, we do not have to have the gift of healing in order to heal others in Jesus' name.

Even if we are not particularly gifted in an area, we can still become proficient if we devote time to practice. We can all heal in Jesus' name. This is part of our inheritance as followers of Jesus. Healing is part of our journey of discipleship. But if we want to become proficient in healing others, learning, growth, willingness to try and fail, and lots of practice are necessary.

Viewing healing only through the lens of a spiritual gift is incorrect. Instead, we must think in terms of spiritual training. We can all learn to do the things called spiritual gifts. Those who are truly gifted in these areas simply find it uncommonly easy.

Conclusion

In this chapter we have seen that healing was part of Jesus' discipleship curriculum. He taught his followers to heal the sick and then sent them out to heal. We have also seen that healing is included in the Great Commission. When Jesus commissioned his followers prior to his ascension to heaven, he expected them to heal the sick. Finally, we have seen that we do not have to have the gift of healing to heal the sick.

Key Bible Passage

> After this the Lord appointed seventy-two others and sent them two by two ahead of him to every town and place where he was about to go. He told them, "The harvest is plentiful, but the workers are few. Ask the Lord of the harvest, therefore, to send out workers into his harvest field...
>
> "...Heal the sick who are there and tell them, 'The kingdom of God has come near to you.'" (Luke 10:1–2, 9)

Teaser

But what about God's will? Where does God's will fit into the matter of healing? What if it is not God's will to heal? We'll answer these questions in the next chapter.

Closing Prayer

Lord Jesus, I thank you that you are not a God who withholds good things from us. You are not withholding your healing power. You long to pour it out on your people. But Lord, much of the time we don't understand the importance of practice. Your first disciples practiced, and they became proficient. Help us to practice too. Help us not to get discouraged during our journey of learning.

Chapter Four
If It Be Thy Will
Does God Desire Our Healing?

> *Wrong belief: God wills for some of his beloved children to be sick.*
>
> *Biblical truth: God desires our healing. Some things happen in the world that are not God's will.*

Praying for Spencer

Spencer had stage IV cancer. Several operations, radiation, and heavy doses of chemotherapy had not prevented the spread to other parts of his body. Before I prayed, I explained to the family that I didn't know what would happen when I prayed. I told them that I would invite the presence of God, rebuke the illness, and then ask him how he felt.

After I prayed, several other family members prayed. Each prayed a heartfelt prayer for Spencer's healing. Each ended their prayer with, "Lord, please heal him if it is your will. If not, we accept whatever you have for us." While the submission to God's will demonstrated here is commendable, is this the approach we ought to take when praying for healing? In other words, is sickness ever God's will for us?

Identifying Our Assumptions

Most people reading this book do not doubt that God can and sometimes does heal. Any person who has ever prayed for the recovery of a loved one must believe that God, at least sometimes, heals people today. They ask, "Is it always God's will to heal?" Behind their question is an unspoken assumption: *If it is God's will for my loved one to be healed, then he will recover.* In this chapter we will do two things. First, we will answer the question of whether it is always God's will to heal. Second, we will examine the validity of this assumption: *If it is God's will to heal, then my loved one will recover.*

Before we dive in, I want to acknowledge that in this chapter we will wrestle with subjects that theologians have wrestled with for centuries. As I present my understanding of Scripture, I invite you to join me in wrestling through the issues. You may not land in the same place I have landed theologically, but I hope you will at least be able to see that my position is a valid way to look at the scriptural data. If by the end of this chapter you both catch a glimpse of the love of God for his children and also view the will of God from a slightly different vantage point, then I will have done my job.

Question: Is It Always God's Will to Heal?

The Headache Left

Sujit had a headache. He came into my office wanting me to pray for him. My mentor had recently taught me that before I pray for someone, I should ask God what he wants to do in this particular case. So, I put my hand on Sujit's shoulder, closed my eyes, and dutifully asked the Lord what he wanted me to do. I got a strong sense that God wanted this headache gone. I then prayed with authority, rebuking the headache. After the prayer, I asked Sujit how he felt. He replied, "The headache went away as soon as you put your hand on my shoulder."

There might be many things to learn from this event, but one thing I learned was that God is eager to heal. Still, the question remains: "Is it always God's will to heal?"

Jesus Demonstrated God's Will

Jesus' life demonstrated what was on the heart of the Father. Indeed, he only did what he saw the Father doing (John 5:19).

> When Jesus came down from the mountainside, large crowds followed him. A man with leprosy came and knelt before him and said, "Lord, if you are willing, you can make me clean."
>
> Jesus reached out his hand and touched the man. "I am willing," he said. "Be clean!" Immediately he was cleansed of his leprosy. (Matthew 8:1–3)

Jesus explicitly stated his willingness to heal. We see the same willingness in action a few verses later. "When Jesus had entered Capernaum, a centurion came to him, asking for help. 'Lord,' he said, 'my servant lies at home paralyzed, suffering terribly'" (Matthew 8:5–6). According to Matthew, Jesus didn't even wait for the centurion's request. Jesus was so desirous to heal that he offered to make the journey to the centurion's house even before being asked to do so (v. 7).

When Peter's mother-in-law was sick, no one had to beg Jesus to heal her. "When Jesus came into Peter's house, he saw Peter's mother-in-law lying in bed with a fever. He touched her hand and the fever left her, and she got up and began to wait on him" (Matthew 8:14–15). All Jesus needed was to see the sickness of someone who was dear to him, and he stretched out his hand and healed her.

After Jesus learned of the death of his friend and cousin John the Baptist, he went by boat to a solitary place to process his grief. But still the crowds came to him. "When Jesus landed and saw a large crowd, he had compassion on them and healed their sick" (Matthew 14:14).

The biblical text is clear. Jesus demonstrated that he was willing to heal the sick. There is no recorded case of a person who came to Jesus but did not receive healing. Matthew stops to make the point that healing the sick was bound up in who Jesus was: "This was to fulfill what was spoken through the prophet Isaiah: 'He took up our infirmities and bore our diseases'" (Matthew 8:17).

Since the disposition to heal was part of his nature, it makes little sense to assume that Jesus' readiness to heal only lasted while he was on earth and does not continue now when he is positioned at the right hand of God (Ephesians 1:20; Acts 7:55) and always interceding for us (Romans 8:34; Hebrews 7:25).

Since Jesus is "the image of the invisible God" (Colossians 1:15) and since "God was pleased to have all his fullness dwell in him" (Colossians 1:19), we can rest assured that God the Father always desires our healing as well. He has the same disposition. It is the Father's will to heal the sick. God demonstrated what his will was regarding sickness through Jesus.

If we take the apostle John's prayer for his dear friend Gaius as an inspired expression of the will of God, then it is not God's will for us to be sick. "Dear friend, I pray that you may enjoy good health and that all may go well with you, even as your soul is getting along well" (3 John 2). Good health is what God desires for us, not cancer or some wasting disease. I know this flies in the face of what many Christians, including me for many years, believe. Yet, I just cannot find clear teaching anywhere in the Bible that God wants his children to be sick.

Counterarguments

There are a number of counterarguments to the idea that God always desires our healing. We will look at two in this chapter and one in the next.

Counterargument 1: God Allows Sickness for Our Good, Just Like Paul's Thorn

Margaret's Story

Margaret had a number of health issues. When I asked Margaret about her view of sickness and healing, she said, "I know that God heals, though I haven't experienced it myself." So far, so good. Then she went on to add, "God lets things like sickness happen because he can see that it is for the person's good." Margaret cited Paul and his thorn in the flesh as an example of this. So, what was Paul's thorn and how does it relate to sickness?

Paul's Thorn in the Flesh

Paul refers to his thorn in the flesh immediately following a description of a man (most likely him) who was caught up into heaven and heard wonderful things that he was not permitted to tell.

> Therefore, in order to keep me from becoming conceited, I was given a thorn in my flesh, a messenger of Satan, to torment me. Three times I pleaded with the Lord to take it away from me. But he said to me, "My grace is sufficient for you, for my power is made perfect in weakness." Therefore I will boast all the more gladly about my weaknesses, so that Christ's power may rest on me. That is why, for Christ's sake, I delight in weaknesses, in insults, in hardships, in persecutions, in difficulties. For when I am weak, then I am strong. (2 Corinthians 12:7b–10)

As a result of these "surpassingly great revelations" (v. 7a), Paul was given a thorn in his flesh to keep him from becoming conceited. Many commentators assume that Paul's thorn was either a sickness or physical handicap of some sort.[1] Some have postulated that it was eye trouble which made it difficult for him to write by his own hand.[2] But was Paul's thorn a sickness?

In verse 7, the thorn is referred to as a tormenting messenger of Satan. The Greek word translated as "messenger" is *angelos*.[3] Excluding the passage quoted above, this word is used at least 180 times in the Greek New Testament. Of these, 167 times the word means angel, six times it means human messenger,[4] and seven times it refers to a fallen angel or demonic spirit.[5] This word is never once used in the New Testament to refer to a non-sentient entity such as disease.

Second, the word "thorn" is used in the Bible several times to figuratively refer to a troublesome person.

> "'But if you do not drive out the inhabitants of the land, those you allow to remain will become barbs in your eyes and thorns in your sides. They will give you trouble in the land where you will live.'" (Numbers 33:55 See also Joshua 23:13 for the same usage.)
>
> "'No longer will the people of Israel have malicious neighbors

---

1. A typical commentary entry suggests an eye problem, physical weakness, speech problem, multiple sclerosis, or stroke along with depression and temptation as possibilities for Paul's thorn in the flesh. See, for example, Got Questions Ministries' "What Does 2 Corinthians 12:7 Mean?"

2. Paul wrote with large letters (Galatians 6:11), and he made a point of writing the closing greeting of his epistles himself (1 Corinthians 16:21; Colossians 4:18; 2 Thessalonians 3:17; Philemon 19). However, it is never stated that this was due to eye trouble. It could be that this was his characteristic way of writing.

3. *Mickelson's*, s.v. "G32 aggelos." This word is usually transliterated as *angelos*.

4. Matthew 11:10; Mark 1:2; Luke 7:24; 7:27; 9:52; James 2:25.

5. Matthew 25:41; 2 Corinthians 11:14; 2 Peter 2:4; Jude 6; Revelation 9:11; 12:7; 12:9.

who are painful briers and sharp thorns. Then they will know that I am the Sovereign Lord.'" (Ezekiel 28:24)

We have, therefore, no clear biblical grounds to state that the thorn Paul referred to was a sickness.[6] Rather, the thorn in Paul's flesh that God used to keep him from being conceited was most likely either another person or a direct attack from an evil spirit. Certainly, the truth that Paul went on to declare in the following verse, "My grace is sufficient for you, for my power is made perfect in weakness" (2 Corinthians 12:9), is relevant during times of sickness. But we are on unstable ground theologically to claim that our sickness is a thorn in our flesh given to keep us from being conceited.

We have dealt with one counterargument. Let's go on to look at another.

Counterargument 2: God Is Testing Me like Job

What about the testing of Job? Didn't God test Job with sickness? Might our sickness be part of a grand test of our faith? Let's look at what the book of Job actually says:

> One day the angels came to present themselves before the Lord, and Satan also came with them. The Lord said to Satan, "Where have you come from?"
>
> Satan answered the Lord, "From roaming throughout the earth, going back and forth on it."
>
> Then the Lord said to Satan, "Have you considered my servant Job? There is no one on earth like him; he is blameless and

---

6. I am not the only one who holds this view. I recently came across an article by Frank Viola which adds further detail to my argument. See Viola's "Rethinking Paul's Thorn in the Flesh."

> upright, a man who fears God and shuns evil."
>
> "Does Job fear God for nothing?" Satan replied. "Have you not put a hedge around him and his household and everything he has? You have blessed the work of his hands, so that his flocks and herds are spread throughout the land. But now stretch out your hand and strike everything he has, and he will surely curse you to your face."
>
> The Lord said to Satan, "Very well, then, everything he has is in your power, but on the man himself do not lay a finger."
>
> Then Satan went out from the presence of the Lord. (Job 1:6–12)

It wasn't God who tested Job, it was Satan. Satan believed that Job only followed God for his blessings, and if the blessings were taken away, then Job would turn his back on God. When Job proved Satan wrong, Satan was quick to up the ante.

> "Skin for skin!" Satan replied. "A man will give all he has for his own life. But now stretch out your hand and strike his flesh and bones, and he will surely curse you to your face."
>
> The Lord said to Satan, "Very well, then, he is in your hands; but you must spare his life." (Job 2:4–6)

Satan was the one who afflicted Job with sickness, not God. It was not God's intention to bring suffering on Job and it is not God's intention to bring suffering on us. We see God's true intention at the end of the book of Job. There we read that the "Lord restored his fortunes and gave him twice as much as he had before" (Job 42:10). "The Lord blessed the latter part of Job's life more than the former part. He had fourteen thousand sheep, six thousand camels, a thousand yoke of oxen and a thousand donkeys" (Job 42:12). God desired his blessing and his health, not his sickness. This time-limited sickness was Satan's attack. It was not God's will that Job suffer in sickness, it was Satan's will. Yes, God allowed Job's sickness just as he allows many other evil things to happen in the world, but it was not his will.[7]

As the book of James shows us, the correct exegesis of Job is not to look at any sickness or trial through the lens of God testing us. Rather, the correct exegesis of Job, as interpreted by James in the New Testament, is that we should hold on to our faith and wait with patience for God to vindicate us.

> Brothers and sisters, as an example of patience in the face of suffering, take the prophets who spoke in the name of the Lord. As you know, we count as blessed those who have persevered. You have heard of Job's perseverance and have seen what the Lord finally brought about. The Lord is full of compassion and mercy. (James 5:10–11)

But could it be that Satan is afflicting me too, just like he afflicted Job? Absolutely! It is highly likely that Satan and his army of demons are seeking to afflict you just like they afflicted Job. Satan is your enemy. The Bible tells us that Satan has been cast down from heaven (Revelation 12:9; Luke 10:18) and that he is waging war against those who keep God's commands and hold to the testimony of Jesus (Revelation 12:17). This situation is not unique to Job or you; it is the daily experience of those who walk close to the Lord.

However, our situation in salvation history is different from Job's. Jesus has now triumphed over death at the cross. As disciples of Jesus, just like the

---

7. If you can't understand how something can happen apart from the will of God, just hang on until the next section. We are going to deal with that very issue.

seventy-two, we have been given authority "to overcome all the power of the enemy" (Luke 10:19).

Assumption: If It Is God's Will to Heal, Then My Loved One Will Recover

Jesus demonstrated our loving heavenly Father's heart. It is his desire that we be healed. This is his will. Paul's thorn in the flesh cannot be used to justify our sickness, neither can the testing of Job. But questions remain: If it is God's will to heal, then why isn't everyone healed? If it is not God's will for us to be sick, then why do we still struggle with sickness? Why is not everyone immediately healed the moment we pray for them? These questions reveal an underlying assumption: If it is God's will for my loved ones to be healed, then they will recover.

As we saw in our introductory example, many people append "if it be thy will" to the end of their prayers. They assume that if their prayer is according to God's will, then they are guaranteed to get what they ask for. But is that the way it works?

There are many factors that impact the effectiveness of our prayers. Faith is one (Mark 11:22–24). Earnestness is another (James 5:17). Authority and power are others (see chapters 7 and 8 in this book). The fact that we pray for something that is God's will is not a guarantee that the prayer will be answered.[8]

When Jesus taught his disciples to pray, he said, "This, then, is how you should pray: 'Our Father in heaven, hallowed be your name, your kingdom come, your will be done, on earth as it is in heaven'" (Matthew 6:9–10). The clear implication of this passage is that God's will is not always done on earth.

---

8. I realize my statement here appears to contradict 1 John 5:14–15. But we must allow the rest of Scripture to inform our understanding of this passage. For example, in Matthew 17:14–20 it was clearly God's will for the child to be delivered from a demon, yet the disciples could not drive the demon out, despite their best efforts.

If God's will were always done, then it would be meaningless to pray for it to be done.

Despite this prayer being prayed by millions of people daily, any national newspaper will conclusively prove that God's will is not always done on earth. In today's *Daily Star* newspaper, I found stories of murder, kidnapping, drug dealing, misappropriation of government assets, fraud, malnutrition, and disease.[9] Things such as these are clearly not God's will, yet they happen on a regular basis.

The Bible teaches us that God is patient with us, "not wanting[10] anyone to perish, but everyone to come to repentance" (2 Peter 3:9b). Statisticians tell us that worldwide 166,859 people die each day.[11] A large percentage of these perish into eternity without receiving salvation through Jesus. This is also clearly contrary to God's expressly stated will.

Our only rational conclusion is that many things happen that are not according to the will of God, and sickness is one of these. We know that our omnipotent God is sovereign. He has the power to do anything he wants to do. But God has chosen not to control the outcome of every single event that happens on earth.

A Disturbing Thought

The idea that God does not control all events is disturbing for some Christians. If God doesn't control everything, then what will happen to the world? Those troubled by this thought may find some relief when they understand that there is a difference between God's will (what he desires will happen but what often

---

9. *The Daily Star*, October 2, 2021. https://www.thedailystar.net/. Two days prior, the reporting was similar, with the addition of rape.

10. The Greek word translated as "wanting" in the NIV refers to God's will. *Mickelson's*, s.v. "G1014 boulomai."

11. See "How Many People Die Each Day in 2024?," World Population Review.

does not happen) and his eternal purpose (that which cannot be thwarted (Ephesians 3:11)).

The death and resurrection of Jesus for the salvation of humankind is an example of something within the eternal purpose of God (Acts 2:23). Christians such as Euodia and Syntyche living together in harmony (Philippians 4:2), rulers governing in a way that allows us to live peaceful and quiet lives of godliness (1 Timothy 2:1–3), and Christians living so as to win the respect of outsiders (1 Thessalonians 4:10–12) are examples of the will of God—events that God desires to happen but which often do not.[12]

Nevertheless, the concept that God's will is not always done in the details of our lives is hard for many Christians to accept. They believe that since God is all powerful, his will is always done. But this is just not true. It is not true because he has delegated authority to his people. Specifically, Jesus delegated his healing ministry to those who followed him. As a result, control over disease depends to a large extent on how we, Jesus' followers, respond to the delegated task we have been given. We will see how this works in subsequent chapters.

Conclusion

Jesus abundantly demonstrated that it is God's will to heal. Jesus never turned away anyone who came to him for healing. Yet when people do not experience healing, they frequently cite Paul's thorn in the flesh. But as we have seen, there is no indication in the text that the thorn is a sickness. People also cite the sufferings of Job, but Job's sufferings were caused by Satan's attack, not by God. Now, because of Christ's victory at the cross, we have authority over all the power of the enemy (Luke 10:19).

If it is not God's will that we are sick, why are people still sick? People are still sick because God's will is not always done. God's will is not done because God's people do not corporately rise up and do it.

---

12. R. C. Sproul unpacks three facets of God's will in "Discerning God's Will."

Many people are paralyzed in their prayers because they don't know if it is God's will to heal. God's will is clear. He desires your healing. Don't let doubts about whether or not God wills healing hold you back. If you want to be healed, pursue healing! If you want to minister healing to others, go for it!

Key Bible Passages

> This was to fulfill what was spoken through the prophet Isaiah:
>
> "He took up our infirmities
> and bore our diseases." (Matthew 8:17)
>
> "This, then, is how you should pray:
>
> 'Our Father in heaven,
> hallowed be your name,
> your kingdom come,
> your will be done,
> on earth as it is in heaven.'" (Matthew 6:9–10)

Teaser

The idea that God has a purpose in every event that befalls our lives, whether good or evil, is so deeply ingrained in the Christian psyche that we will look at this concept in depth in the next chapter.

Closing Prayer

Lord Jesus, your will is recorded in your written word, the Bible. There, by both example and teaching, you made it clear that it is your will that we be healed. Oh Lord, help us to rise up and do it.

Chapter Five

Doesn't God Have a Purpose in My Sickness?

Looking at God's Sovereignty and His Control

> *Wrong belief: God controls all things, therefore the bad things, including sickness, that happen to us must have a beneficial purpose behind them.*
>
> *Biblical truth: When we walk with God, he can bring good even out of the bad that happens to us.*

A Gift from God?

When I asked Chuck whether he would like prayer for his sickness, he responded that he had tried this earlier. Before his cancer operation more than a decade earlier, friends from his church anointed him with oil and prayed for him. The cancer remained and Chuck underwent life-altering surgery. Chuck told me that in the intervening years he had learned to see his suffering as a gift from God given to make him more like Jesus.

Was Chuck's cancer a gift from God given to develop his character or was it the result of sin and suffering entering the world as a result of the fall? Or worse, was this cancer an attack from the pit of hell, ultimately sent by Satan the destroyer?

A Cure for Stubbornness?

Kara had fibromyalgia and several other health issues. When I offered to pray for her, Kara refused. The conversation went as follows.

Kara: God allowed this sickness to teach me to depend on him.
Neil: Would you wish this sickness on your children?
Kara: No. I would not wish this kind of pain on anyone. But God knows I am very stubborn.
Neil: Are your children not stubborn?
Kara: Yes. They are.

Even though Kara said that her children were stubborn, she would not wish sickness on them to cure them of their stubbornness. How then could our loving heavenly Father visit us with sickness to cure us of our character faults? Despite my reasoning, I could not convince Kara to allow me to pray for her. Her theology created a barrier. If Kara followed her reasoning to its logical conclusion, she would never go to a doctor or take medicine for her health issues.[1] If God willed her to be sick to teach her some spiritual lesson, then she would be acting contrary to God's will if she took medication to relieve her suffering.

---

1. I am indebted to Smith Wigglesworth for this idea. See *Ever Increasing Faith*, 42–43.

A Challenge to Make Us Grow?

Daniel was no stranger to chronic pain. He had been struggling with back pain for years, and now, frozen shoulder. We were sitting in another friend's backyard, talking about healing. Daniel was willing for us to gather around and pray for him. His wife was the first one to pray and she prayed with passion. After her prayer, she wiped tears from her eyes. There was no change in Daniel's condition. I then prayed for Daniel a couple of times without seeing any change. The third time, I began with, "Lord we know that you do not want Daniel to be suffering in this way." Then I stopped and asked, "Daniel, do you believe this?"

"I know that God wants me to be well eventually, one day in heaven." But Daniel was not at all sure that God wanted him to be well now. He asked, "What if God wants me to learn something through this period of suffering?"

"Would you wish a disease on your son to teach him a lesson?"

"No."

"How can you think your heavenly Father would do the same for you?" We then talked about how challenge is necessary for growth in both academics and athletics. In athletics, for example, some tolerance of pain is required.

Daniel responded, "I firmly believe this to be true."

"But you don't hit your son with a hammer to teach him to tolerate pain."

Daniel ended with, "I'll have to think about that one."

The Source of Evil

No parent in her right mind would wish cancer, fibromyalgia, or any other sickness on her child, even if it was for a positive end such as increased maturity. No good parent would injure their child in order to provide a challenge leading to growth. To do so would be cruel. Parents who are cruel have their children removed from them by the state. If your children were rebellious, your heart would grieve, but you would not wish a terrible, wasting disease on them. Sickness came from the fall. It is not God's will for us.

Jesus tells us, "The thief comes only to steal and kill and destroy; I have come that they may have life, and have it to the full" (John 10:10). If we see destruction in our lives, we can pinpoint the source: Satan, not God.

God Works All Things for Good

Chuck and Kara looked for some redeeming element in sickness. They assumed that the hand of God was behind their sickness, and therefore the appropriate response was to accept the sickness with equanimity. Where do we get the idea that God brings evil into our lives? It may come from an incorrect understanding of a very familiar passage of Scripture. Since "all things work together for good" (Romans 8:28 KJV), it is assumed by many that God brings all things into our lives. But does he?

Theologian David Guretzki explains:

> Not everything has a purpose. That may be shocking to read from the pen of a theologian, but let me explain.
>
> The text often cited for the idea everything has a purpose is Paul's declaration, "We know that all things work together for good to them that love God, to them who are called according to his purpose" (Romans 8:28 KJV). I affirm the claim of this wholeheartedly. But does this verse really say everything has a purpose?
>
> To affirm God works out everything according to His purposes is very different than saying everything—every event, every tragedy, every mystery, indeed every evil and sin committed in this world—has a God-ordained purpose.

As a perfectly good and holy God, He will not and cannot ordain evil things to happen. To do so would be a contradiction of His nature.[2]

In Luke 13:10–16 Jesus set a woman free who had been bound by Satan for eighteen years. God didn't bring that evil into her life, Satan did. Acts 10:38 tells us that Jesus "went around doing good and healing all who were under the power of the devil, because God was with him." These verses show us that God is not the source of our sicknesses, the devil is. We are in a struggle against the forces of darkness. To attribute our sickness to the hand of God completely misrepresents our loving heavenly Father. God is not the source of the bad things that happen in our lives and we should not waste time seeking a beneficial purpose in them.[3]

Ignoring sickness for a moment, let's look at bad things in general, and whether or not God is behind them.

A Stolen Car and a Stubbed Toe

One Saturday I spent the day at church as part of a spiritual freedom weekend. When I came out of the building at the end of the day, I discovered that my borrowed car had been stolen from the church's parking lot. This event caused inconvenience and stress to me. Certainly, this event was an opportunity for me to grow and become more Christlike. It was an opportunity for me to trust God in the midst of uncertainty and lack. And yes, things worked out together for

---

2. Guretzki, "Not Everything Has a Purpose."

3. John G. Lake, a man anointed with tremendous healing power, said, "Like a flash from the blue, these words pierced my heart: Oppressed of the devil! So, God was not the author of sickness! And the people whom Jesus healed had not been made sick by God!" Lake, *Adventures in God*, 79.

good for me—I was loaned a much nicer car. But God didn't cause the car to be stolen. A gang of thieves that frequented the nearby mall, motivated by the powers of darkness, stole it. Even though things turned out well for me, they did not turn out so well for the owner of the car—a fellow member of the same church. He eventually found his car, abandoned in a mall parking lot. But there were several hundred dollars' worth of damage done, not to speak of the hours of wasted time.

If I were to come out of the church and find the thieves in the process of breaking into the car, I would not sit idly watching them steal it so that I would have an opportunity to become more Christlike. Instead, I would burst out of the church shouting to scare the thieves away, or I would call the police and hope they arrive quickly enough to catch the hooligans in the act.

Similarly, walking barefoot in my house and stubbing my big toe on the table leg is not a pleasant experience. Clenching my teeth so that I don't say something inappropriate and not allowing my mind to go into a pain-induced spiral of negative thinking is a difficult step towards Christlikeness. Nevertheless, it is inappropriate to say that God caused me to stub my toe. I will, in future, be careful to avoid repeating that mistake.

Even though I can grow as a result of negative events—and I will grow if I keep in step with Jesus—I must not credit God as the source of the negative events.

Is Suffering a Means to Our Redemption?

The unbiblical concept that we should passively accept suffering as redemptive has long been in the Christian tradition. During Martin Luther's day, the concept that suffering was redemptive had reached such an extreme that monks regularly whipped themselves.[4] Historian William De Arteaga tells us:

---

4. Nathan Busenitz, "The Personal Reformation of Martin Luther." See also Wikipedia's "Self-flagellation."

The early monastic movement was also captivated by the Stoic concept that pain and illness were to be accepted bravely, and without striving for healing....An absolute connection was made between the sufferings brought on by illness and the believer's sharing of Christ's sufferings. This concept of illness as redemptive suffering subordinated the many Scripture passages which showed that illness was brought on by demonic oppression and an evil to be countered by the church's ministry (Luke 13:16, for example).[5]

God doesn't send suffering to redeem us. Jesus redeems us, not our suffering. We are transformed by Jesus as we walk with him through all the events of our lives, whether good or evil. As we walk with God, he can and often does bring good out of our bad. As Pastor Paul Manwaring says, "The mistake people make is that God is so good at turning bad stuff into something beautiful that people think he sent it."[6] But this does not mean we should simply accept the bad things that happen.

Suffering can cause us to cast ourselves so completely upon God that we become more like Jesus. But that does not mean that God sends the negative events. Satan does not need God's help in that department. Nor does this mean we should welcome all suffering as God's instrument to make us more Christlike. Jesus came "to destroy the devil's work" (1 John 3:8); we must not passively accept it.

---

5. De Arteaga, *Agnes Sanford and Her Companions*, 19.

6. As quoted in *Paid in Full*, directed by Art Thomas and James Loruss. Quote starts at 1:12:30.

Does Sin Prevent Healing?

In the next chapters we will look at several reasons why we often do not see the level of healing we desire. In this section, we will work through a touchy subject: does sin prevent healing?

What about the Curse of Sickness in the Old Testament?

Earlier, we looked at Kara. Could Kara's sickness be due to her sin? In Deuteronomy 28 the Israelites were told, "If you do not carefully follow all the words of this law, which are written in this book, and do not revere this glorious and awesome name—the Lord your God—the Lord will send fearful plagues on you and your descendants, harsh and prolonged disasters, and severe and lingering illnesses" (v. 58–59).

Might then our sickness be due to our sin? In response to this, we must note several things. First, the old covenant with its rules and regulations, including the blessings and curses set out in Deuteronomy, has been set aside and is therefore no longer in force (Hebrews 8:7–9a). Although it is possible to argue that the Mosaic covenant reflects God's character, and therefore principles of blessing and cursing found in Deuteronomy apply to us today,[7] we must be cautious about making a direct connection between sickness and sin. Jesus did not make such a connection (John 9:3).

Second, even if the Deuteronomy passage linking sickness to sin still applies to us, we must note that the sin referred to in Deuteronomy is not simply making minor mistakes in fulfilling all the details of the Mosaic law. The sin referred to here is the sin of turning away from the living God and worshiping idols (Deuteronomy 28:14; 29:25–28). This is rebellion against the Lord of Hosts—a life direction away from God.

---

7. There is much debate in the Christian world regarding what to do with the Old Testament law. For a short summary of the many different options, see Wikipedia's "Christian Views on the Old Covenant."

Third, even if this part of the old covenant still applies, there is a simple cure: "return to the Lord your God and obey him with all your heart and with all your soul" (Deuteronomy 30:1–10; see also 2 Chronicles 7:13–14). God made it clear that under the old covenant, the cure for the Israelites' problems was to turn back to the Lord and then he would restore their fortunes. Thus, if Kara's sickness was due to some sin in her life, all she would need to do is repent of any specific sin that the Lord brought to mind and come back to the Lord.

In summary, a genuine Christian who has asked for forgiveness for known sin in their life and who, as best as they understand, is seeking to walk in obedience to the Lord, cannot claim that God will not heal them because their sickness has arisen because of their sin.

No Prerequisites for Healing (Usually)

Jesus healed crowds of people, many times simply by speaking a word (Matthew 8:3, 8, 13, 16). Surely, among the hundreds or thousands of people he healed, there must have been some who had serious sin issues. Yet Jesus did not require them to get spiritually cleaned up before they came for healing. At the pool of Bethesda, Jesus healed a man who had been an invalid for thirty-eight years (John 5:2–9). There was no record that Jesus dealt with any sin issue prior to his healing. But when they met again later, Jesus said to him, "See, you are well again. Stop sinning or something worse may happen to you" (v. 14). Jesus' words imply that the man did have a sin problem, yet Jesus didn't make cleaning up his life a prerequisite for healing. Unless we have a very clear word from the Lord, we shouldn't either.

Sickness Is an Impetus to Seek the Lord

The biblical record shows us that in some, but certainly not all cases, the sin and rebellion of certain individuals caused sickness to come into their lives, yet Jesus did not make repentance a prerequisite for healing. Where does that leave us? The following examples will show us the way forward.

Asa's Foot Disease

Asa, king of Judah, smashed the idols and sacred stones set up by his ancestors. When the Cushites marched against Judah, he relied on the Lord and experienced the Lord's deliverance (2 Chronicles 14:2–13). About two and a half decades later, Asa faced military opposition again. This time instead of relying on the Lord, he relied on money for his deliverance. When the prophet Hanani rebuked him, he got angry and put him in prison. Asa also began to oppress some of his people (2 Chronicles 16:1–10).

Three years later, Asa contracted a severe disease in his feet. Although the Bible does not link this disease to his sin, the Bible does tell us that Asa did not seek the Lord for healing, he only sought help from physicians (2 Chronicles 16:12). If Asa had sought the Lord, the Lord would have brought him face-to-face with his heart issues, his pride and oppression. We can view sickness as an impetus to seek the Lord on a deeper level.

Hezekiah's Illness

Many generations after Asa, King Hezekiah also became sick to the point of death. Unlike Asa, Hezekiah earnestly sought the Lord with tears. The result was that God healed him (2 Kings 20:1–7).[8] Rather than seeing sickness as the necessary result of sin, or as an aspect of the inscrutable will of God, it is better to see sickness as an impetus to seek the Lord on a deeper level.

---

8. Some argue that it would have been better for Hezekiah not to have prayed for his own healing because in the latter part of his life he became proud and he fathered a son who was very evil. I disagree with this logic. Hezekiah's prayer was appropriate given the situation he faced. The fact that he later became proud is a separate issue and also a warning to us. If God blesses us, let us be careful to continue to follow the Lord in humility.

The Headache That Wouldn't Leave

My friend Jonathan and I had just spent ninety minutes ministering to Joanne, a woman who had been suffering from severe demonic attacks. Near the end of our ministry session, I asked Joanne how she was feeling. She said that she had a headache. Both Jonathan and I rebuked the headache, but it did not leave. Instead, it moved to pain behind the eyes.

The time I had allotted for this ministry session was running out and I was thinking that I was going to be late for my next appointment that evening. I wanted a quick solution. As I was asking the Lord what to do, I received a mental picture of James, Joanne's husband, with his hand on Joanne's head, praying for her. I was not sure what this vision meant but wondered if it meant that James would need to learn how to minister to his wife after we left.

I encouraged James to pray for Joanne, but he refused. After a bit of probing, he admitted that he didn't want to pray because, he said, "I am sinful." I told him to ask God to show him the sin, confess it, and then pray for her. Finally, James told us that he was unwilling to forgive his father for the severe beatings he had received in childhood. I explained that forgiveness is a choice—like choosing to cancel a debt. Eventually, he forgave his father. As soon as he did so, Joanne's headache left.[9] The headache served as an impetus for us to seek the Lord on a deeper level.

Dealing with the First Item on God's Agenda

The following fictitious story illustrates an important principle of prayer ministry and rounds out the idea that sickness can serve as an impetus to seek the Lord on a deeper level.

---

9. It seems that the spirit causing the headache was in some way related to the fact that James would not forgive his father. My guess is that lack of forgiveness on James' part opened a door of access for an evil spirit to trouble his wife with a headache.

Frank's Migraines

Frank was struggling with migraines and desired relief from his malady, so he came to Johnson for prayer. Unknown to Johnson, Frank also had a secret addiction to pornography. Frank was ashamed of his sin and felt like garbage. All his attempts to get freedom through self-control had failed. He went to a pastor once, but the pastor only made him feel more guilty. Now Frank was too ashamed to mention his problem to anyone.

Johnson prayed with all his might for Frank's migraines, but nothing changed. With our knowledge of Frank's sin, it would be easy to make a straight cause-and-effect connection: Frank is living in sin; therefore God will not heal him. However, if we make such a connection, we turn Christianity into a clean-yourself-up-before-you-get-God's-blessings reward for good performance. This is not the way our relationship with God works. We come to him with all our sinfulness. God meets us where we are at. God's gracious gifts are not contingent on our spiritual performance.

So why wasn't Frank healed when Johnson prayed? Let's view the situation from God's perspective. God wants Frank to be healed of his migraines. God also wants Frank to be healed of his deeper and more serious pornography problem. Let's assume that God wants to deal with the heart issue before he addresses the physical pain. To encourage Johnson and Frank to probe a little deeper, God temporarily withholds his healing power. As both Johnson and Frank ask the Lord why healing has not occurred, God leads them to the first item on his agenda: facing the woundedness in Frank's heart that causes him to turn to pornography for solace. Being in tune with God's agenda in each encounter with a sick person will lead to greater effectiveness in healing.[10]

---

10. We need, however, to be cautious and kind. We cannot assume that heart issues are always the reason why a person is not healed.

Conclusion

Some people say that God gives sickness to teach us a lesson or to shape us into Christlike character, but this is not congruent with the loving heart of God. Certainly, we face difficulties in this life. May we learn and become more Christlike in every difficulty we face. But the fact that we can learn from our painful situations doesn't mean we should sit passively by when a difficulty comes. Like Jesus, we are called to destroy the works of the devil.

The Bible does record specific occasions where individual sickness was linked to individual sin, but individual sickness is not always caused by individual sin. If sickness is the result of sin, we can simply ask God to reveal the sin, and then turn to him in repentance. As we pray for people, we need to pay attention to what the first item on God's agenda is. Jesus healed many people without dealing with their sin problem first, but in other biblical accounts, we see that healing came after dealing with heart issues. We can view sickness is an impetus to seek God more deeply.

Key Bible Passages

> "You know what has happened throughout the province of Judea, beginning in Galilee after the baptism that John preached—how God anointed Jesus of Nazareth with the Holy Spirit and power, and how he went around doing good and healing all who were under the power of the devil, because God was with him." (Acts 10:37–38)

> "When I shut up the heavens so that there is no rain, or command locusts to devour the land or send a plague among my people, if my people, who are called by my name, will humble themselves and pray and seek my face and turn from their

wicked ways, then I will hear from heaven, and I will forgive their sin and will heal their land." (2 Chronicles 7:13–14)

Teaser

In the next chapter we will examine the concept of human agency. We will find out why God's will is not always done on earth as it is in heaven.

Closing Prayer

God, I thank you with all my heart that you are a good God. Thank you that you do not cripple or injure us to reform our character or make us grow spiritually. I thank you again that you desire our healing.

Chapter Six

Once Upon a Time, There Was a Great King

The Role of Human Agency in Healing

> *Wrong belief: God does what he wants to do without our involvement.*
>
> *Biblical truth: God works in partnership with his children. We are co-regents with God.*

Zorba's Problem

Once upon a time, in a country far away, there was a great and beneficent king. His subjects adored him because they knew he sought the best for them. One day, Alexander, a devoted and loyal subject, came to the king with a problem. Alexander's brother, Zorba, lived in the country and farmed his own land. But Zorba's enemies constantly tormented him. They thought that if they bothered him enough, he would move elsewhere, allowing them to take over his home and fields.

Alexander came into the king's magnificent throne room. The floor was covered in plush carpet. The walls were draped in red and gold. Heavy curtains hung over the doors and windows. The paintings on the ceiling depicted the exploits of the king's ancestors. Beside the king stood his royal officials, his servants, and several heavily armed soldiers, all ready to carry out the king's commands. Alexander bowed low before the golden throne and spoke on behalf of his brother. He described how Zorba's enemies burned his crops, threw garbage into his house, and threatened to harm his children. After hearing Zorba's plight, the king was moved with compassion.

Did the great king come down from his throne, personally travel to Zorba's house, and punish Zorba's enemies? Of course not. "Go and deal with those scoundrels," said the king to Alexander. "Go in my authority and arrest those men. If they don't listen to you, don't hesitate to draw your sword. Free your brother from his torment. And take this contingent of soldiers with you, to make sure those evil men heed your command."

The king gave orders to Alexander to act on his behalf.

In my allegory, we are Alexander. The soldiers are angels. God is the great and beneficent king. Zorba is our brother or sister tormented by sickness. Many times, like Alexander, we beg God, our great and beneficent king, to heal our sick friend. God, however, is waiting for us to use the authority he has already given us to bring healing.

I imagine God on his throne looking on his petitioning servants with a measure of sadness. "If only they would listen to me as much as they plead with me. Why can't they understand that I have made them co-regents with me? Don't they know that thousands of angels are on hand to help them?[1] I have given them authority to act on my behalf. Why don't they just pluck up the courage to go and deal with the problems they are facing? Why don't they drive out the sickness in my name as I have commanded them to do?"

---

1. Hebrews 1:14.

That's a nice little allegory, you say, but it doesn't prove anything. How do we know that God does indeed rule through agents such as you and me? This is such an important concept that we will deal with it at length.

God Rules through Agents

An agent is "a person who acts on behalf of another person or group."[2] Let's look at some examples of human and angelic agents in the Bible.

Old Testament Examples of Human Agents

God commanded the first humans to subdue the earth and to rule over all its creatures (Genesis 1:28). This was their task. God was not going to do it for them. Neither was God going to tell them what to do at every step of the way. They were to be God's agents on the earth.

When the Hebrews were mistreated in Egypt, they cried to God for deliverance. God could have sent a wasting disease to destroy the entire Egyptian population. He could have supernaturally caused the Israelites to become instantly free. Instead, God called stammering Moses and told him, "See, I have made you like God to Pharaoh, and your brother Aaron will be your prophet" (Exodus 7:1). Moses was God's agent, acting on his behalf before Pharaoh.

God gave the land of Canaan to the people of Israel. They were to take possession of this land (Joshua 1:11). God could have annihilated the inhabitants of the land and given them an empty country to dwell in. But he didn't. He wanted them to drive out the inhabitants of the land and demolish all signs of the idolatry they used to practice (Numbers 33:51–53). They were to exercise authority as the new legal owners and possess the land. They were to act. They were to be God's agents bringing judgment on the Canaanites (Genesis 15:16).

When the Midianites impoverished the Israelites "like swarms of locusts," the Israelites prayed to God for help (Judges 6:1–6). God could have sent fire from

---

2. "Agent." Oxford Languages, Oxford University Press.

heaven on the marauding Midianites and put an end to the problem. Instead, he chose Gideon to deliver the Israelites from the suffering they were experiencing (Judges 6:14). Gideon was God's agent to bring deliverance to Israel.

New Testament Examples of Human Agents

In the New Testament we also see people acting on God's behalf. Jesus began his ministry proclaiming the good news of the kingdom of heaven and healing the sick (Matthew 4:23–25). Then Jesus sent his disciples to do the very same thing (Matthew 10:1–8). The disciples, imbued with Jesus' authority, went out and acted on his behalf, healing the sick, raising the dead, and proclaiming the kingdom. They were his agents.

One of the most important spheres of human agency is found in the Great Commission (Matthew 28:18–20). God could very well have preached the gospel to the whole world without us. He doesn't need us to reveal himself to humankind. He revealed himself to Moses at the burning bush (Exodus 3:1-6). He revealed himself to Saul the persecutor through a vision on the Damascus road (Acts 9:1–6). He can act without our involvement. But this is not God's preferred way of doing things. He wants to work with us. He wants us to go out on his behalf.

> And he has committed to us the message of reconciliation. We are therefore Christ's ambassadors, as though God were making his appeal through us. We implore you on Christ's behalf: Be reconciled to God. (2 Corinthians 5:19b–20)

This is a crazy but true concept. The awesome God of the universe, the God who can do absolutely anything, has chosen to work through us. He has chosen us as his agents to accomplish his will in the world.

Paul tells us that "God raised us up with Christ and seated us with him in the heavenly realms in Christ Jesus" (Ephesians 2:6). Note that Paul uses the past tense in this passage. He is not talking about something that will happen in the coming age; he is talking about what has already happened. If God has already "made us alive with Christ even when we were dead in transgressions" (v. 5), then we are already seated with Christ in the heavenly realms. Reigning with Christ—co-regency—this is the heart of being God's agent. God desires to work through his people and through them establish his kingdom on earth.

What It Means to Be Part of God's Kingdom

The kingdom of God is a prime example of God ruling through agents. Before we can see this, however, we must understand what Jesus meant when he used the term "kingdom of God."[3] I used to think of God's kingdom as primarily a future state into which those who had received salvation through Jesus would enter. Jesus' use of the term was far broader than this.

Jesus taught his disciples to pray that God's kingdom would come (Matthew 6:9–10). Jesus was not only talking about some future hope, he was talking about the kingdom of God coming in their lifetimes, into the very lives of those who prayed this prayer. The fact that Jesus drove out demons was proof that the kingdom of God had already come near his hearers (Matthew 12:28). Even though the kingdom of God was present and available to them, not all of Jesus' hearers became part of the kingdom.

So, what did Jesus mean when he spoke of the kingdom of God? Theologian Dallas Willard defines God's kingdom as follows.

> God's own "kingdom," or "rule," is the range of his effective will, where what he wants done is done. The person of God himself and the action of his will are the organizing principles

---

3. Matthew primarily uses the term "kingdom of heaven" whereas Mark and Luke use "kingdom of God." Many scholars see the terms as interchangeable.

of his kingdom, but everything that obeys those principles, whether by nature or by choice, is within his kingdom.[4]

The kingdom of God is where "what he wants done is done." This only happens when God's people line up their wills with God's will and do what God desires to be done. The kingdom of God has arrived, but we only become a part of it when we obey our king and fulfill his wishes. When we are part of the kingdom, God expresses his rule through us. We serve as his agents, carrying out his will on earth.

Spirits Are Agents of God

God doesn't only rely on human agents to do his will. Angels also serve as his agents (Matthew 4:11; Matthew 26:53; and Luke 22:43). Daniel 10 records how an angel came in response to Daniel's prayers. Apparently, God did not directly respond to Daniel's request; he dispatched an angel. That angel encountered a difficulty while bringing Daniel an answer. He was obstructed for three weeks by the prince of the Persian kingdom—presumably a powerful evil ruling spirit assigned to the kingdom of Persia (Daniel 10:12–14). The first angel was not successful in bringing an answer to Daniel until yet another angelic agent, Michael, came to the first angel's assistance.

Characteristics of Agents

God executes his will through agents, both human agents and spirit agents. There are three important characteristics of agents related to the application of human agency in healing. Let's look at them now.

---

4. Willard, *The Divine Conspiracy*, 25.

Agents Are Limited in Power

Since agents are not omnipotent, they may not possess sufficient power to carry out God's will in a given situation. Daniel's angel was not able to defeat the prince of the Persian kingdom by himself. This angel needed Michael's assistance. Likewise, as we go out to bring God's will into a situation, we may not have sufficient power to do what needs to be done. We may need to join together as a combined force with other agents of the kingdom.

The disciples could not deliver a boy from a spirit that made him mute (Mark 9:17–29). They lacked sufficient power and authority. Later, when they had time to talk, they came to Jesus and asked why they were not successful in casting the spirit out. Jesus responded, "This kind can come out only by prayer" (v. 29). As we will see in subsequent chapters, time spent in personal and corporate prayer increases our power and authority. Agents are not omnipotent; they are limited in power.

Agents Have Great Flexibility in How They Act

When God told Gideon to cut down his father's idol, Gideon had a choice as to exactly how he would do this. Out of fear, he chose to do it at night, and he took ten people with him to help (Judges 6:25–27). He had freedom in the timing and whether he did it alone or with others.

Saul was anointed by God through Samuel to be the first king of Israel. Samuel prophesied that certain signs would confirm that he was indeed to be the king. Then Samuel told him, "Once these signs are fulfilled, do whatever your hand finds to do, for God is with you." (1 Samuel 10:7) Saul was appointed to be God's agent, to rule over the people of Israel, but God did not tell him what to do in every detail. He could do whatever his hand found to do—whatever was appropriate in a given situation. He had great freedom and flexibility in how he would function as God's agent.

Likewise, when we go to heal a person, there are different ways that we can go about it. We may pray loudly or under our breath. We may or may not anoint with oil. We may go alone or with others. Agents have freedom and flexibility in how they act.

Slave-master relationships do not give room for personal autonomy. Partnerships do. God has called us from slavery to the position of heir (Romans 8:15). We are coworkers with God (2 Corinthians 6:1), and as a result, we enjoy a large degree of personal freedom.

Agents May Choose Not to Act

Agents are not robots. They have their own will. Even when they have the authority and power to act, they may not choose to do so. Jesus did not heal all the sick people at the pool of Bethesda (John 5:1–9). Peter and John did not heal all the beggars in the temple (Acts 3:1–8). When Jesus sent out the Twelve, he told them, "Do not go among the Gentiles or enter any town of the Samaritans. Go rather to the lost sheep of Israel" (Matthew 10:5–6). This was not because the power and authority they had been given wouldn't work among the Gentiles and Samaritans. Rather, it was because Jesus wanted them to focus their ministry at this point on the people of Israel.

When faced with overwhelming crowds of people, there were times when Jesus chose not to act. "When Jesus saw the crowd around him, he gave orders to cross to the other side of the lake" (Matthew 8:18). Jesus was intentionally choosing not to minister to more people in this crowd.

When the Lord gives us his power, it is not always appropriate to pray for every sick person we encounter. Sometimes our time is better spent in communion with him or teaching and training a smaller group.

On the other hand, sometimes we ought to act, but choose not to do so. The Lord may bring a person across our path who needs the Lord's touch, but we may be too lazy or too fearful to exercise the authority we have been given.

Implications of the Fact That God Rules Through Agents

While visiting with my friend Edgar over lunch, we began to talk about healing. Edgar expressed a sentiment commonly held among Christians: "God sometimes heals people and sometimes doesn't and we don't understand why." On the one hand, I agree with Edgar that we do not know why some people are healed and others are not. On the other hand, maybe the issue is not that God isn't healing, but that we aren't acting with the authority we have been given.

We are agents of God assigned to act with his authority. We are his co-regents, tasked with reigning with him now. Much of what God desires to be done is not done because we, his agents, simply don't do what we have been given to do. Pastor Jordan Seng expresses it this way:

> For example, we know we shouldn't wait around for God to preach to the unreached, because that's our job. So, we pray about it and learn Scripture and study missiology and practice preaching like good soldiers. In a similar way, we shouldn't just wait around for God to heal the sick; we should lay hands on and heal them directly, and we should be working aggressively and diligently to become good healers. But if we convince ourselves that supernatural ministries should be left entirely to God, then we won't invest in preparing to do them, and then we'll be in no shape to try them when the time comes.[5]

It is primarily through agents, both human and spirit, that God accomplishes his will. As agents, we must act. Much spiritual work does not happen because God's agents do not act with the authority they have been given.

---

5. Seng, *Miracle Work*, 42–43.

Acting with Agency

It was May 2020. Bangladesh was enduring a country-wide "general holiday"[6] and many people were showing symptoms of COVID-19. Testing was hard to come by and vaccines had not been invented yet. No one really knew how serious the disease was. Schools and offices were closed and people who had the technology to do so were working from home.

The little house church that we were a part of was meeting online. One week, Rozina requested prayer. Both Rozina, a follower of Jesus, and her husband Robiul, a Muslim, had been sick with high fevers for four or five days and were feeling weak and tired. After the meeting, I got Rozina's phone number through a mutual friend, called her up, and prayed for her and her husband.

Rozina quickly recovered over the next few days, but her husband did not. Six days later I heard that he was terribly sick, had difficulty breathing, and was very weak. They were planning to go to the hospital the following morning if his condition did not improve.

Knowing that hospitals in many countries are not pleasant places for the poor, I was concerned that Robiul would get worse if he were taken to one. As I prayed about the situation, I felt that God was inviting me to go to their home and pray for Robiul. I did not hear God commanding me to go, rather, I understood that God would be pleased if I went.

The next morning, I called Rozina, found out where they lived, and hopped on my motorcycle to go to their house. When I arrived, I found Robiul sleeping on the bed, the piece of furniture which occupied most of their one-room dwelling. Rozina told me that Robiul had been having a lot of pain in his chest and that he had been coughing blood. He hadn't had solid food for three days. Rozina, however, looked well and told me that she was perfectly fine. She had recovered after the prayer over the phone six days earlier.

She woke Robiul and he sat up on the bed. When he saw me, he scooted into the far corner so as to not spread the contagion. I told him that I wanted to put

---

6. "General holiday" was the government's *nom de guerre* for "lockdown."

my hand on him and pray for him. I sat beside him on the bed and began to pray. I put my hand on his chest and rebuked pain, sickness, COVID-19, and anything else I could think of to rebuke.

After the prayer he told me that he felt good, but that he felt very weak. I understood that the pain had gone but that his strength hadn't returned. I put my hand on his shoulder and prayed for him to receive strength. After this prayer he coughed. Then he looked at me and said, "There is no pain." Again, he told me that he felt good. A week later, at the house church online prayer meeting, Rozina effusively praised God because Robiul had recovered.

After receiving God's invitation to visit Robiul, I acted with agency. I went to their house and prayed for him and he was healed. What would have happened if I had not gone?

Conclusion

God rules through agents as do all rulers. God could do everything himself, but he has chosen to carry out his will through created beings, both human and spirit.

We are partners with God, working together with him. We are not simply slaves or robots who can only carry out orders. He graciously gives us his authority and his power and then bids us go and do exploits in his kingdom. As God's agents, we can affect the environment around us. We can minister healing. We must choose to act. If we do not, many people who could be healed will not be.

Key Bible Passage

> And God raised us up with Christ and seated us with him in the heavenly realms in Christ Jesus. (Ephesians 2:6)

Teaser

Agents must be imbued with both authority and power if they are to carry out their king's orders. In the next two chapters, we will look at these two concepts.

Closing Prayer

Lord, I thank you for making me a co-laborer with you. You have seated me in the heavenly realms with Jesus. This is such an amazing concept that I can hardly get my head around it. Lord, help me to know, deep within my heart, that I have agency, that I have a role to play, that I am called to act on your behalf. Oh Lord, let me not be a passive Christian, one who sits back and begs you to do what you have commanded me to do.

Chapter Seven

The Fearless Policeman

A Study in Authority

> Wrong belief: We do not have authority over sickness.
>
> Biblical truth: We have been given great authority and we need to learn to use it.

Dhaka Traffic

I was heading out for my evening run. Traffic was moving in full swing at the major intersection near our house. As usual, three lanes of southbound cars were crowding through the intersection. The police officer on duty was no scaredy-cat. After several minutes, he blew his whistle, held out his baton, and began walking in front of the stream of moving cars. The drivers reluctantly brought their vehicles to a halt. The officer then pointed to the three lanes of waiting northbound vehicles and motioned for them to proceed.

In Bangladesh, where traffic lights are routinely ignored, it takes a clear demonstration of authority to make traffic stop. Even when the officer has indicated with his hand that a lane of vehicles should stop, most do not respond until the officer begins walking in front of the cars. There are always a few vehicles in the far lane who defy the officer's authority and scoot through the intersection before he gets to them. The drivers know that there are not enough police on duty to chase them down for such a minor infraction and so the risk of any consequences for denying authority are small.

The police officer stops cars through the exercise of his authority. But why do the cars stop at all? The power of even a small car is greater than the physical power of the largest policeman on duty. Why don't the drivers just run over the policeman and keep on going? Because the level of disregard for authority involved in killing a police officer would invite severe consequences.

In the spiritual realm both power and authority play important roles and they work similarly to the way they work in the visible realm. If we are going to be effective in ministering healing, we must understand the concepts of power and authority. In this chapter we will look at authority. In the next, we will examine power.

Defining "Authority"

The Greek word translated as "authority" is *exousia*.[1] This word carries both the idea of the authority to tell another person what to do[2] and the right to do something personally.[3] Below we examine several principles of authority. These principles apply equally in the visible and spiritual realms.

---

1. *Mickelson's*, s.v. "G1849 exousia."

2. See, for example, the uses of authority in Matthew 8:9; 10:1; and 20:25.

3. See 1 Corinthians 9:5, where Paul talks about his right, i.e., his authority, to have a wife.

Principle 1: We Must Be under Authority If We Are to Exercise Authority

Except in the case of an absolute monarch, an overriding principle of authority is that you must be under the authority of a person or group to exert authority over a person or group. This is clearly illustrated in the case of the centurion who came to Jesus on behalf of his sick servant.

> When Jesus had entered Capernaum, a centurion came to him, asking for help. "Lord," he said, "my servant lies at home paralyzed, suffering terribly."
>
> Jesus said to him, "Shall I come and heal him?"
>
> The centurion replied, "Lord, I do not deserve to have you come under my roof. But just say the word, and my servant will be healed. For I myself am a man under authority, with soldiers under me. I tell this one, 'Go,' and he goes; and that one, 'Come,' and he comes. I say to my servant, 'Do this,' and he does it." (Matthew 8:5–9)

Being a part of the hierarchical Roman military system, this centurion knew that he had authority, and that those he commanded must obey or face serious consequences. But he also knew that he only had authority because he was under the authority of Rome. If he were to desert from the military, he would instantly lose all his military authority. We operate under the authority of the person we submit to. Observing Jesus, the centurion realized that Jesus was also part of an authority structure. Within that authority structure, Jesus gave orders to disease and spirit beings, and they obeyed him instantly.

The principle that one must be under authority to exercise authority was well understood by the Jews in Jesus' day. When the religious leaders questioned

Jesus after he cleansed the temple, they wanted to know under whose authority he was operating.

> Jesus entered the temple courts, and, while he was teaching, the chief priests and the elders of the people came to him. "By what authority are you doing these things?" they asked. "And who gave you this authority?" (Matthew 21:23)

Being under authority means being obedient to the authority over us. Ken Blue, reflecting on Israel's victory at Jericho after obeying God's instructions, and their subsequent defeat at Ai after disobedience (Joshua 6–7), says:

> This very clear connection between obedience and authority, and disobedience and the lack of authority, leads me to believe that the relative lack of authority in the healing ministry in the Western church is not only due to an inadequate theology and inappropriate models, but also due to the moral corruption, unbelief and disobedience in our corporate body. Leslie Weatherhead suggests that, "it may well be that the whole fellowship of the church needs to be raised to a higher spiritual level today before individual healers in it can repeat the healing activities of the Son of God."[4]

The first principle is that we need to be under authority if we are to exercise authority.

---

4. Ken Blue, *Authority to Heal*, loc. 1413 of 1544, Kindle.

Principle 2: Authority Is Exercised by Command

The centurion understood that authority is exercised by command. "I tell this one, 'Go,' and he goes" (Matthew 8:9), he said. The centurion then said that all Jesus needed to do was "just say the word, and my servant will be healed" (Matthew 8:8). Indeed, that is what Jesus did and the servant was healed. Later in the same chapter we read that Jesus "drove out the spirits with a word" (Matthew 8:16). Authority is exercised by command.

Many people spend much time in intercession, sometimes even begging God for the healing of their loved ones. Intercessory prayer plays an important role in the life of the Christian, but it is not what Jesus and the apostles did when they ministered healing. They commanded healing, and the healing occurred according to what they commanded. Although there are some biblical references to prayer in the context of healing, we observe that people recovered, not after the request was made to God, but after the command was given to the patient or to the sickness.

> Peter sent them all out of the room; then he got down on his knees and prayed. Turning toward the dead woman, he said, "Tabitha, get up." She opened her eyes, and seeing Peter she sat up. He took her by the hand and helped her to her feet. Then he called for the believers, especially the widows, and presented her to them alive. (Acts 9:40–41)

Tabitha didn't come to life when Peter prayed. She came to life when Peter commanded her to get up. We see the same thing in Paul's life on the island of Malta.

> There was an estate nearby that belonged to Publius, the chief official of the island. He welcomed us to his home and showed us generous hospitality for three days. His father was sick in bed, suffering from fever and dysentery. Paul went in to see him and,

> after prayer, placed his hands on him and healed him. When this
> had happened, the rest of the sick on the island came and were
> cured. (Acts 28:7–9)

Publius's father didn't recover when Paul prayed. He recovered when Paul did an authoritative act—when Paul placed his hands on him. Prayer can help to bring us to a place where we are confident to act with authority, but when we know our authority, we don't even need to pray. Most of the healings recorded in the Bible were done simply by command, without even a preparatory prayer. (For just a few of many examples, see the healings recorded in Matthew 8:3, 8–13, 16; 9:6; Acts 3:6; 9:34; 14:8–10). Prayer is best done at home when you are alone. You don't need to pray in the traditional sense of making a petition to God when you minister healing. All you need to do is issue a command.

Although we frequently say things like, "I prayed for healing for Jeffrey," in many cases it would be more accurate to say, "I ministered healing to Jeffrey," particularly when we issue a command to a body part to be whole in Jesus' name.

Our second principle is that authority is exercised by command. If we do not grasp this concept, we will be limited in our effectiveness in healing.

Principle 3: Authority Can Be Delegated

If we are in a position of authority, we can delegate authority to others. A king can send an emissary to act on his behalf. Ministers in a parliamentary system are endued with authority over their portfolio. A CEO delegates authority to the VPs of each division in her company. The same principle applies in the spiritual realm. Authority can be delegated and Jesus delegated authority to his disciples.

> Jesus called his twelve disciples to him and gave them authority
> to drive out impure spirits and to heal every disease and sickness.
> (Matthew 10:1)

Later, Jesus delegated authority to seventy-two others. The seventy-two were shocked at the results. Even when they didn't fully understand the extent of their authority, they could use the authority they had been given. On their return, with joy they exclaimed, "Lord, even the demons submit to us in your name." (Luke 10:17). Jesus' response further clarifies the amount of authority that has been delegated to them and to us.

> He replied, "I saw Satan fall like lightning from heaven. I have given you authority to trample on snakes and scorpions and to overcome all the power of the enemy; nothing will harm you." (Luke 10:18–19)

After Jesus ascended into heaven, Peter and John faced an unusual request in Samaria for the delegation of authority.

> When Simon saw that the Spirit was given at the laying on of the apostles' hands, he offered them money and said, "Give me also this ability so that everyone on whom I lay my hands may receive the Holy Spirit." (Acts 8:18–19)

The word translated as "ability" here is *exousia*, meaning "authority." Simon wanted authority to confer the Holy Spirit and, based on his sinful understanding of the way the spiritual realm worked, offered money to get this authority. Simon was right in his understanding that authority can be delegated. He was terribly wrong in trying to purchase this authority with money.

Since authority is frequently conferred through the laying on of hands (Numbers 27:18–23), Paul advised Timothy not to be hasty in this practice (1 Timothy 5:22). Although Paul's advice to Timothy was in the context of the formal ordination of leaders, laying on of hands, when done by a person with genuine authority in the spiritual realm, seems to have the effect of transferring spiritual authority to another person.

Jesus reiterated the idea of delegated authority in the Great Commission. "All authority in heaven and on earth has been given to me. Therefore go and make disciples of all nations" (Matthew 28:18–19). Jesus has been given all authority. He then delegated authority to us and he expects us to use it.

Principle 4: We Can Grow in Authority

Not everyone has the same amount of spiritual authority. We readily understand this in the natural realm. The level of authority of a traffic police officer is far different from that of a senior judge. The authority of an army general is greater than the authority of a captain. In the spiritual realm, we see that the apostles had high levels of authority. Great signs were performed by them (Acts 2:43). But they did not start off their walk with Jesus with this level of authority. When the disciples were in a boat in a storm, instead of using the authority available to them, they panicked (Matthew 8:23–26).

Jesus told a story about a member of nobility granting authority over large sums of money to his servants while he traveled to a distant country (Luke 19:11–26). On his return, the nobleman, now king, rewarded those who had used their authority wisely by giving them even greater authority. For example, the king said to one of his servants, who had earned ten minas in his absence, "Well done, my good servant!...Because you have been trustworthy in a very small matter, take charge of ten cities" (Luke 19:17). Another servant, who had earned five minas in the king's absence, was given charge over five cities. Their increase in authority was in proportion to how effectively they had used the authority previously given to them.

This story shows that we have great freedom in the use of the authority that has been delegated to us. We can determine how we use it. We can choose not to use it in certain instances or choose to never even use it at all. This story also shows us the path to growing in authority. As we use the authority we have been given, God will give us more.

Using My Authority in Deliverance

A pastor took me to the hostel connected to his church because I wanted to pray for one of the sick boys there. While I was ministering to the sick boy, the pastor saw another boy go into a trance. Soon the second boy's trance turned into an all-out demonic manifestation. While I and a couple of the more experienced boys held the demonized boy down, the pastor commanded the demons to leave.

Feeling that I was a novice at this type of deliverance ministry, I let the pastor take the lead. The demon, however, was not in a mood to leave quietly. The boy struggled, his eyes rolled back into his head, and he made a lot of noise. The boy, or rather the demon or demons inside, cried out, "I won't go. I will return. You will not be able to drive me out." My first response was to laugh at the demon and tell it that it was lying. After a while I got tired of this, and yelled, "Shut up." To my surprise, the demon obeyed. Immediately there was silence. I used the authority I had and, as a result, grew in my authority.[5]

Why Don't We Walk in Our Authority?

I was new in my role as the director of a development project in Bangladesh. In my twenties, I was also very young in a society that respected the aged. Under me were two Bangladeshi coordinators, both of whom were older than I. Under them were several area supervisors and a number of field workers, bringing the total number of employed staff to around twenty people.

Since I was new in the country, and had much to learn about local culture, I relied heavily on my coordinators to help me make decisions. Usually we functioned as a three-person leadership team. However, problems arose when

---

5. If I were to encounter a similar situation again, I would want to handle things differently. First, I would command silence. Then I would ask the Lord what the point of entry was. Based on what the Lord showed me, I would command the demon behind that sin or oppression to leave. Afterward, I would seek to help the boy to close any open doors so that demons would no longer have access through those points of entry.

the decisions were about personal favors for my coordinators. One came to me each year requesting that his annual bonus be given to him early. In the first few years, I didn't have the guts to say, "No. You will take your bonus on the same date as all the other staff." What should I do when my two coordinators came to me with the request that I increase their salary? They outvoted me two to one. It didn't immediately occur to me that I had the authority to veto their requests.

Another day, some of the junior staff made an error in the distribution of food on a special day when local officials had been invited to visit the project's activities. When it came time to eat, there was not enough food for the officials. Back in the office later that day, the coordinator, justifiably upset over the shame this incident brought upon the project, soundly rebuked his staff. In that context, a rebuke was appropriate. The problem was, this coordinator wouldn't stop. After the berating had gone on for fifteen minutes, I wanted everyone to go home and forget the incident. Further talk would not change what had happened. I didn't realize that I had the authority to say, "Enough. You have scolded them long enough. They understand their mistake. Now keep silent and let the staff go home." Even if I had realized my authority, I wouldn't have had the courage to use it. What if the coordinator defied me in front of all the staff? Fear of personal embarrassment prevented me from walking in my authority.

We can't walk in our authority when we don't know that we have it. We won't walk in our authority if we are afraid that it won't work.

Using My Authority in Healing

Jibon and his wife, Shanti, had arrived in Bangladesh several months previously, but Shanti was plagued with sickness much of the time they were here. One particularly troubling issue was neck and shoulder pain. Since we had recently returned from home assignment, this was our first time to meet them as a family in their new home. I thought Ingrid, my wife, a physiotherapist, was going to treat her neck. But since Shanti was already getting physiotherapy elsewhere, and it seemed to be helping, Ingrid made no move to begin treatment.

I wondered if I should pray for her. I had a sense of God's presence, so I offered to pray. Shanti then described her symptoms in more detail: pain in the shoulder and chest area, numbness in her arm, and depression. I asked her to tell me her level of pain on a one-to-ten scale. She said the level was around five. The range of symptoms suggested to me the possibility of a demonic attack.

I put my hand on her shoulder and prayed. I invited the Lord's presence to come and then I quietly rebuked the pain and underlying problems. After this, I prayed for the Holy Spirit to come and touch her. It seemed apparent that the Lord had indeed touched her.

When the prayer was over, I asked her to move around and check out the shoulder. She had a look of surprise on her face and told us that the pain was almost all gone. She looked happier too.

I used the authority given me to bring healing to Shanti. If we want to effectively heal others, then we need to understand the principles of authority.

Conclusion

Commanding healing and rebuking sickness and demons are the primary methods of ministering healing demonstrated in the Bible. There is no record of Jesus ever praying for a sick person. He healed by command, by demonstration of authority. Similarly, in private, the disciples prayed that God would stretch out his hand to heal (Acts 4:30), but in public they healed by command.

We must also learn to use the authority we have been given. Suppose the police officer we referred to at the beginning of this chapter was a scaredy-cat. Suppose he had not learned that he actually had the authority to stop traffic. Suppose he simply stood at the side of the road and timidly blew his whistle. The cars in Dhaka would ignore him and continue their uninterrupted flow. Likewise, if we do not use the authority we have already been given, we will not be able to heal others.

Key Bible Passages

> The centurion replied, "Lord, I do not deserve to have you come under my roof. But just say the word, and my servant will be healed. For I myself am a man under authority, with soldiers under me. I tell this one, 'Go,' and he goes; and that one, 'Come,' and he comes. I say to my servant, 'Do this,' and he does it." (Matthew 8:8–9)

> Then Jesus came to them and said, "All authority in heaven and on earth has been given to me. Therefore go and make disciples of all nations, baptizing them in the name of the Father and of the Son and of the Holy Spirit, and teaching them to obey everything I have commanded you. And surely I am with you always, to the very end of the age." (Matthew 28:18–20)

Teaser

In September 2021 in Mount Carmel, Pennsylvania, a man in possession of drugs, a knife, and an imitation gun resisted arrest. He was ordered to place his hands behind his back, but he refused. The officers involved, finding that their authority was not sufficient to obtain compliance, began to apply other tools at their disposal. They used pepper spray and physical force to handcuff the man and place him in the police cruiser.[6] In the spiritual realm as well, we may at times find that authority isn't sufficient; power must be utilized. To be effective in a healing ministry, we need to have both authority and power. We will examine the concept of spiritual power in the next chapter.

---

6. Gilger, "MC Man Charged with Resisting Arrest."

Closing Prayer

Lord Jesus, you have all authority in heaven and on earth. And you have delegated this authority to us. You want us to go out with the authority we have been given and do the things you have commanded us to do. Lord, I confess that I have not acted in this authority because I didn't know that I had it. At times, I have not acted in my rightful authority as a child of the king because I was too scared to do so. But no more. Lord, from this day forward, I want to act in my authority.

Chapter Eight
Spiritual Dynamite
What the Bible Says About Power

> *Wrong belief: Spiritual power does not reside in human beings.*
>
> *Biblical truth: God has promised to give us his power.*

Make Me an Amulet

The weekly church service in Barishal is usually an informal affair. By the time everyone arrived one week in October, we were twelve adults sitting on reed mats placed on the hard concrete floor. Koli had only come once before. But this time she brought her daughter, Shima, with her. Shima's husband had left her two years ago for another woman and so Shima was left to raise their two children alone. Her six-year-old boy wandered around during the meeting while her four-year-old girl, who was sick, remained in Shima's lap.

The service started with some rusty singing. Since the chosen speaker hadn't come, I was asked to teach. I gave an impromptu message on forgiveness. During the service, I asked those present, "Have any of you been harmed by another person?" Most admitted they had. Unknown to me, the Bengali word I was using for "harmed" meant "cursed" in the local dialect. Most of those present said that someone had placed a curse upon them. They believed in the power of spoken curses.

At the end of the service, several of us prayed for the sick child. When it was my turn to pray, I felt an unction rising within me. Not only did I pray for the child, but I prayed for Shima as well. With authority, I declared any curses spoken over this young mother to be broken. (A few days later, I heard that the child had recovered.)

After the meeting was over, Koli, functionally illiterate, asked me to write some words on a piece of paper for her. I knew what she meant. She was asking me to make an amulet that would protect her from harm. Amulets in Bangladesh usually consist of words or numbers written in Arabic and then sealed in a tiny metal canister and tied with string around one's arm or waist.

When I gently refused, Koli persisted, saying, "Why not? Don't you know Arabic?" She knew that words have power, and I had demonstrated power when I spoke authoritatively over her daughter to break curses. She wanted me to put some powerful words on a piece of paper that she could keep with her for protection.

In this folk Islamic culture replete with tales of holy men able to both effect cures and inflict diseases, most Bangladeshis know that some people have power. The way to share in this power, they believe, is to submit themselves to a holy person.[1]

Power and Miracles in the Bible

As evangelicals, we recoil from the idea that power can be resident on a person or object and that the person or object imbued with the power can provide a

---

1. It is commonly believed that one way to draw power into oneself is to touch the feet of a holy person, hence the custom of touching the feet of an elder or someone who is believed to possess more power than oneself.

tangible blessing to another. We are afraid that acknowledging the existence of such power will lead to worship of something or someone other than God. We are right to be cautious about who or what we worship, yet in our attempts to avoid error, we may end up denying the existence of legitimate spiritual power and that we can be carriers of it.

I want to acknowledge that some readers may find the concepts in this chapter difficult to accept because they run counter to commonly held beliefs. As I did at the beginning of this book, I would only ask that you continue reading and see if I can produce biblical evidence to support my assertions, and then pray and reflect on the teaching, asking the Lord if he has anything he wants you to learn here.

Power Is Not the Same as Authority

The Greek word translated as power is *dunamis*. This word has a range of meanings, such as power, bodily strength, ability to do something, capacity, and capability of acting.[2] We see *dunamis* reflected in English words like dynamite, dynamic, and dynamo.

If I were to point to a picture of former German Chancellor Angela Merkel and say, "She was a powerful woman," I would be referring to her authority. If I were to point at a picture of Muhammad Ali, the boxer, and say, "He was a powerful man," I would be referring to his bodily strength. In English, "power" has a range of meanings, including both physical strength and relational authority. In the Greek New Testament, *dunamis* also has a range of meanings, but this range only rarely, if ever, includes the idea of authority.[3]

---

2. Liddell and Scott, *A Greek-English Lexicon*, s.v. "δύναμις."

3. *Mickelson's*, s.v. "G1411 dunamis." The full definition from *Mickelson's* is "n. 1. force. 2. (specially) miraculous power. 3. (usually by implication) a miracle itself." When the Bible uses the plural form "powers" to refer to people or spirits, it seems to be indicating beings that utilize their power to exert influence over others. See Colossians 1:16 for an example of this usage.

Let's look at translations of *dunamis* as found in the English New Testament.

Translations of "Power" in the Bible

One translation of *dunamis* is seen in Luke 5:17: "One day Jesus was teaching, and Pharisees and teachers of the law were sitting there. They had come from every village of Galilee and from Judea and Jerusalem. And the power [*dunamis*] of the Lord was with Jesus to heal the sick." Here *dunamis* refers to the ability to make something happen—in this case, the miraculous act of making a sick person well.

A second translation of *dunamis* is "ability." In Matthew 25:15, in the parable of the talents, each person was given money "according to his ability [*dunamis*]." We see the same meaning in 2 Corinthians 8:3 where we read about the Macedonian Christians who gave "beyond their ability [*dunamis*]."

Another common translation of *dunamis* is "miracle." In John 7:21, Jesus said to the crowd, "I did one miracle [*dunamis*], and you are all amazed." So *dunamis* can be translated as power or ability or miracle.

Humans Doing Miracles

If you, like me, were raised in the church, you probably believe that only God can perform miracles. This, however, is not what the Bible teaches. The Bible consistently demonstrates that humans can perform miracles.

"Humans can perform miracles"—this may come across as a shocking statement. Let's look at the biblical data to see if we find confirmation.

In Matthew 7:22, Jesus, teaching about the kingdom of heaven, said, "Many will say to me on that day, 'Lord, Lord, did we not prophesy in your name and in your name drive out demons and in your name perform many miracles?'"[4] Later on in Matthew, Jesus told his disciples to "heal the sick, raise the dead, cleanse those who have leprosy, drive out demons" (Matthew 10:8). All of these activities fall under the traditional definition of miracle, and yet Jesus commanded his disciples to do them.

In the book of Mark, Jesus explicitly stated that ordinary humans could do miracles.

> "Teacher," said John, "we saw someone driving out demons in your name and we told him to stop, because he was not one of us."
>
> "Do not stop him," Jesus said. "For no one who does a miracle in my name can in the next moment say anything bad about me, for whoever is not against us is for us." (Mark 9:38–40)

Jesus declared that humans can do miracles in his name. Performing miracles, however, requires intentionality. Jordon Seng, in *Miracle Work*, says,

> We shouldn't expect God to drop supernatural healings from the sky any more than we expect him to drop sermons from the sky. Instead, we should expect to work on each of them ourselves, and for God to empower us to do them both.[5]

---

4. I admit that this verse raises some interesting questions because Jesus goes on to say, "I never knew you. Away from me, you evildoers!" I suggest this is an example of people doing God's work with their hearts in the wrong place. For similar examples, see the disciples desiring to call down fire from heaven (Luke 9:54) and Moses, contrary to God's instruction, bringing water from a rock by striking it (Numbers 20:9–12). Apparently, it is sometimes possible to perform a miracle and not be in God's will.

5. Seng, *Miracle Work*, 40.

The Bible is clear that ordinary people can perform miracles. Yet it is so ingrained in our minds that only God can do miracles that the word "miracle" itself can be a stumbling block to us, preventing us from doing what God is calling us to do. To overcome this block, you might find it helpful to replace the word "miracle" with "powerful act" as you read the section below.

Choosing to Perform Miracles

If ordinary humans can perform miracles, the next logical conclusion is that they can decide whether or not they will perform them. Indeed, this is what the Bible demonstrates. Paul believed that miracles were important and so he chose to make a habit of doing them regularly. "I persevered in demonstrating among you the marks of a true apostle,[6] including signs, wonders and miracles" (2 Corinthians 12:12). If we follow the example of Paul, we should proclaim the gospel of Christ "by the power of signs and wonders" (Romans 15:19). Paul chose to demonstrate God's power so that the faith of his hearers would not be based on "human wisdom, but on God's power" (1 Corinthians 2:4–5).

When the Samaritans opposed Jesus, James and John asked permission from Jesus to call down fire from heaven to destroy them. James and John did not doubt their power to accomplish this miracle and Jesus did not tell them they would be unable to do so. Instead, he rebuked them because they did not understand Jesus' mission and sought to destroy people rather than save them (Luke 9:51–56).

Peter and John chose to act with power when they saw the man lame from birth being carried to the temple gate (Acts 3:1–8). They could have walked

---

6. There is debate in the church today regarding whether "apostle" only refers to the Twelve plus Paul, or whether the word has the broader meaning of someone who has been sent on a mission. I won't get into that debate here, but simply note that Barnabas (Acts 14:3–4), Andronicus and Junia (Romans 16:7), Silas and Timothy (pair 1 Thessalonians 1:1 with 2:6), and Epaphroditus (see Philippians 2:25 in Greek) are all called apostles.

right on by and not used the power they had. Instead of ignoring him, however, they healed him.

Stephen, "full of God's grace and power, performed great wonders and signs[7] among the people" (Acts 6:8). Likewise, Philip also performed many signs (Acts 8:4–13). Paul acted with power when he blinded Elymas the sorcerer (Acts 13:6–12). He could have decided that it was too risky to declare that Elymas would become blind. Instead, he acted and performed a miracle of blindness.

Based on what we learned in our study of human agency (chapter 6), we know that Peter, James, John, Stephen, Philip, and Paul weren't robots that only moved when an energizing force inside them made them move. Instead, they were humans, choosing to use their wills to release the power of God that was resident within them. If they had not gone and acted in power, the sick would not have been healed and miracles would not have been performed.

Whose Power Is It?

The beggar healed by Peter and John in Acts 3 was not silent about his healing. Full of joy, he made a great commotion of praise. A crowd quickly formed around the trio and many in the crowd recognized the man who had been healed. Peter addressed the question foremost on their minds: how did Peter and John get the power to heal the crippled man?

> When Peter saw this, he said to them: "Fellow Israelites, why does this surprise you? Why do you stare at us as if by our own power [*dunamis*] or godliness we had made this man walk?" (Acts 3:12)

---

7. The Greek word used here is *semion*, not *dunamis*. But the idea is the same: humans doing miracles.

Then Peter went on to explain that "by faith in the name of Jesus, this man whom you see and know was made strong. It is Jesus' name and the faith that comes through him that has completely healed him, as you can all see" (Acts 3:16). The power is in Jesus' name, but humans are the ones who perform the miracle when the power is activated through faith.

This power resided in Peter, but it was not his own; it was given to him. Peter made it clear that it was not the power of his own human spirit that made the man well. Paul elaborates on the same idea in 2 Corinthians 4:7: "But we have this treasure in jars of clay to show that this all-surpassing power [*dunamis*] is from God and not from us." It is God's power, but this power resides within us.[8]

Is This Power Still Available Today?

That his followers have power after he ascended into heaven was so important to Jesus that he commanded them not to leave Jerusalem until they were "clothed with power from on high" (Luke 24:49). In the book of Acts, Jesus again promised power to his disciples: "But you will receive power when the Holy Spirit comes on you; and you will be my witnesses in Jerusalem, and in all Judea and Samaria, and to the ends of the earth" (Acts 1:8).

This power was not just the power to live a moral life. Nor was it only the power to speak persuasively to large audiences. It was also the power to heal the sick, drive out demons, and perform miraculous signs. If this power is not still

---

8. There are several other places where Paul reiterates the same idea of God's power working in us. See, for example, Ephesians 3:20; Colossians 1:11, 29. Until recently, I understood these verses to refer to God's power in us helping us to live righteous and moral lives. But this is an inappropriate limitation on the meaning of these verses.

available today, then we must cut out the Great Commission passages from the Bible because they include the concept of power.[9]

What Does Power Feel Like?

God's power can be physically perceived when it is in action, either by the one in whom the power is resident or by the recipient of the power. As we see below, sometimes power is perceived as heat. At other times it can feel something like electricity.

Power Perceived as Heat and Electricity

During my university years, I worked in Toronto between semesters. In the evenings, I would kneel on the carpet with my face to the floor and spend long periods of time in prayer. After a while, I noticed that my hands were getting warm. I suspected it was because I was kneeling in front of the floor vent of the heating system. But I checked and, no, the heating system was not running. The warmth was not coming from the vent. I didn't understand it at the time, but God's power was manifesting through a sensation that I perceived as heat in my hands.

One night I resolved that I would not get up from prayer until God touched me.[10] After a period of time, probably not more than fifteen minutes, I sensed what felt like electricity coursing through my body. It was intense, almost to the

---

9. Here are the Great Commission passages and their references to power. In Matthew 28:18–20, "teaching them to obey all that I have commanded" certainly includes the powerful acts of healing. Mark 16:15–20, although disputed by many scholars, echoes the theme of powerful signs. Luke 24:45–49 exhorts the disciples to wait for power. Acts 1:8 explicitly mentions power. John 20:21–22 does not mention power explicitly, but verse 31 teaches that signs are given to lead to belief.

10. I don't recommend making promises like this. Frequently we give up before the answer comes, and then feel guilty about breaking our word. If you want God to touch you, simply ask him to and believe that he will. It is not necessary to make a promise to God.

point where I didn't think I could bear it any longer, yet at the same time, it was a very pleasant sensation, and I didn't want that feeling to stop. It ended after a short time. Although I didn't know what was happening, God was touching me with his power.

Luke tells us that people tried to touch Jesus "because power was coming from him and healing them all" (Luke 6:19). I suspect that many of the recipients of Jesus' touch felt the transfer of power. Jesus was so sensitive to the movements of power that he could tell when power left his body. "Jesus said, 'Someone touched me; I know that power has gone out from me'" (Luke 8:46).

Levels of Power

Each carrier of power is limited. I may have sufficient power in my body to run ten kilometers, but not to run a marathon. My sister-in-law's Toyota Corolla might have sufficient power to drive me through the Rocky Mountains. But it does not have the power to drive through the Rockies towing a two-ton trailer. Only God carries unlimited power.

Some of God's power is resident within each believer. But we do not all carry equal levels of power. The Bible describes Stephen as "a man full of God's grace and power" (Acts 6:8). If everyone had the same amount of power, this description would be meaningless.[11] Even in the case of Jesus, power was not always present within him to the same degree.

> One day Jesus was teaching, and Pharisees and teachers of the law were sitting there. They had come from every village of Galilee and from Judea and Jerusalem. And the power of the Lord was with Jesus to heal the sick. (Luke 5:17)

---

11. Likewise, Paul's opposers did not have the same amount of power that he had. In 1 Corinthians 4:19, Paul says, "But I will come to you very soon, if the Lord is willing, and then I will find out not only how these arrogant people are talking, but what power they have."

The statement that the power of the Lord was present to heal the sick implies that at times the same amount of power was not present.[12] For us as well, our level of power may vary from day to day. Paul carried a great amount of power at the end of his life. "God did extraordinary miracles through Paul, so that even handkerchiefs and aprons that had touched him were taken to the sick, and their illnesses were cured and the evil spirits left them" (Acts 19:11–12).

As we saw in our study of agency in chapter 6, angelic beings also have varying levels of power. Daniel records how he was met by a powerful angel on the banks of the Tigris River (Daniel 10:4–6). This angel had been fighting against the Prince of Persia. However, Daniel's angel was not powerful enough to defeat the Prince of Persia. He was detained until the archangel Michael came to help him (Daniel 10:12–13). If even angels at times lack the necessary power to do what they set out to do, then it makes sense that we at times will come up against the limitations of the amount of spiritual power resident within us.

In the context of healing, we need to understand that healing Stage IV cancer requires more power than healing a headache. We may be full of faith. We may understand our authority, but we may be lacking in the requisite power to do the job.

How Can I Increase in Power?

I used to think that if I fasted and prayed a lot, my spiritual power would increase. Is that true? We'll look at fasting in a moment, but first let's look at prayer.

---

12. See also Luke 4:14, where it says, "Jesus returned to Galilee in the power of the Spirit." This statement implies that prior to this point Jesus did not have the same level of power. The suggestion that at times Jesus was not full of power will be troubling for some. How can the one in whom "the fullness of the Deity lives in bodily form" (Colossians 2:9) ever lack power? Yet we know Jesus also at times became tired and thirsty (John 4:6–7). The power of God could have enabled Jesus not to need rest or nourishment, as it did for Moses for forty days on Mt. Sinai (Exodus 34:28).

Jesus once said to his disciples, "This kind [of demon] can come out only by prayer" (Mark 9:29). However, as we saw at the end of the previous chapter, Jesus never prayed prior to a healing. He healed and delivered[13] by touch and command. The apostles healed in the same manner. When we are full of God's power, we do not need to pray before healing someone either, though we usually do so out of habit and tradition.

So why did Jesus say that this kind only comes out by prayer? Because time spent alone in God's presence increases our spiritual power. Jesus spent a lot of time alone in prayer (Mark 1:35; 6:46) and consequently moved in power. Moses also performed great miracles. What was his secret? He spent so much time in God's presence that the glory of God rested upon him visibly (Exodus 34:29–30). I wonder if the lack of power evident in much of the church today is because many Christians spend very little time in prayer.

Many manuscripts add "and fasting" to the end of Mark 9:29. Does fasting increase the amount of God's power that is resident in us? Maybe, but maybe not. Fasting can be problematic for certain personality types (like mine) because it is easy to turn it into a subtle attempt to manipulate God. *If I fast for a certain number of days, then,* we think, *God is obliged to give me more power.* This kind of thinking is seen in religious belief systems that promote asceticism.[14] Paul himself warned about forms of religion that harshly treat the body (Colossians

---

13. One person told me that deliverance from demons must be done by command only, not touch. Jesus, however, touched a woman who had been bound by an evil spirit and she was delivered (Luke 13:10–16). Note the touch in v. 13.

14. I suspect that ascetic practices coupled with meditative techniques increase the power of the human spirit. This is why ascetic techniques are believed to bring supernatural power. (See "Hindu and Buddhist Asceticism," Encyclopedia.com, which says, "Ascetic techniques in many traditions are said to bring magical or supernatural powers.") We, however, are not seeking to increase the power of our human spirits. We want to be a dwelling place of the Holy Spirit and his power. For Christian ascetics and supernatural powers, see Valantasis, "Constructions of Power in Asceticism." For some stories of miracles in the lives of ascetics, see Allen, "Christian Asceticism."

2:20–22). Fasting in search of spiritual power has not always been a fruitful path for me and I quit fasting altogether for a season.

Longing for God's power, however, is completely appropriate, as Paul demonstrates in Philippians 3:10, where he says, "I want to know Christ—yes, to know the power of his resurrection." Indeed, desiring God's gifts is a principle of God's kingdom (Matthew 7:7–11; Luke 11:5–13; 1 Corinthians 14:1). So how do we grow in power? One way is to ask God for it. The early church did so corporately, and God responded by shaking the building they were in (Acts 4:30–31). Another way is to ask others to pray that we would be filled with power. Paul prayed for the Ephesian believers to be strengthened with power (Ephesians 3:16).

Finally, we must note that God's power comes when the Holy Spirit comes upon us (Acts 1:8). We should therefore constantly seek to be filled with the Holy Spirit. The power of God increases in us when we have a greater anointing of the Holy Spirit.[15]

How Can I Transmit Power to Others?

One primary way of transmitting power, especially the power to heal, is through touch. Mark 16:18 tells us that those who believe will "place their hands on sick people, and they will get well."[16] Jesus touched people often when he was ministering healing (Matthew 9:18; Mark 5:23; 6:5; 7:32; 8:22–25; Luke 13:13).

Power may also be transmitted through words uttered under the unction of the Holy Spirit. Prophecy is the primary example of this form of power transmission, but it can be employed in healing as well (Matthew 8:13, 16).

---

15. There are many places in the New Testament where power and the Holy Spirit are mentioned together. Here is a list: Luke 1:35; 4:14; Acts 1:8; 10:38; Romans 1:4; 15:13, 19; 1 Corinthians 2:4; 12:8–10; Galatians 3:5; Ephesians 3:16; 1 Thessalonians 1:5; 2 Timothy 1:7; Hebrews 2:4.

16. Many commentators suggest that Mark 16:9–20 was not part of the original book of Mark. That may be so, but that does not mean it is not part of inspired Scripture.

Regardless of how the power is transmitted, you must have power before you can transfer it to another person.

Ungodly Power

Christians are not the only ones who seek to access spiritual power. Practitioners of the various forms of energy healing attempt to use the power of the human spirit to effect healing. Energy healing is based on the non-biblical premise that there is a life force in the body called *qi* which needs to be unblocked by ridding oneself of negative emotions.[17] Of course we should rid ourselves of negative emotions. The Bible itself teaches us to do so (Ephesians 4:26; Philippians 4:6–8). And getting rid of negative emotions will invariably have a positive effect on our health. However, the Bible gives no indication that there is such a thing as a life force analogous to *qi*.

Energy healing and similar practices are dangerous because they open a person to the power of the demonic realm. An acquaintance of mine told me that he quit using Reiki (a Japanese form of energy healing) to try to heal others because, as he explained to me, he drew the sickness of the patient into himself and so became sick.[18]

Our spirits do have a certain amount of power.[19] Like physical strength, this is in itself neither evil or good, but it is not the same as God's power.

---

17. For an easy-to-read overview of *qi*, see "Qi," Wikipedia.org. For attempts to measure *qi*, see Ohnishi, "Ki." Despite some people's attempts to merge energy healing with Christian teaching, there is no biblical analog to *qi*.

18. A more accurate way to explain my friend's experience is that his attempts to use spiritual power apart from the Holy Spirit opened him up to demonic attack.

19. Watchman Nee, writing in 1933, identified the problem of relying on the power of the human spirit to do God's work (Nee, *The Latent Power of the Soul*). Although Nee's work is excellent, he mislabels the human spirit as soul.

Conclusion

Power is real and great amounts of it reside on some people. Rather than deny its existence, it is far better to acknowledge that power can rest upon us, but, like Peter and John, credit Jesus as the source of the power. The Holy Spirit (and by extension, his power) is part of the gospel message. Paul warns that in the last days there will be people "having a form of godliness but denying its power. Have nothing to do with such people" (2 Timothy 3:5).

Key Bible Passage

> I pray that the eyes of your heart may be enlightened in order that you may know the hope to which he has called you, the riches of his glorious inheritance in his holy people, and his incomparably great power for us who believe. That power is the same as the mighty strength he exerted when he raised Christ from the dead and seated him at his right hand in the heavenly realms. (Ephesians 1:18–20)

Teaser

In the next chapter we will examine faith, the key that unlocks both authority and power.

Closing Prayer

Lord, I thank you for the power that you have already put in me. I acknowledge that this power is present. I repent of minimizing it and denying it. But, oh Lord, I want more. I pray that you will anoint me with power. Let your power flow out of me so that suffering people receive the healing that you have made available to them through the name of Jesus.

Chapter Nine
But I Have No Faith
Examining What Faith Is and How to Get It

> *Wrong belief: Faith is trying to psych myself up to believe something I don't think will happen.*
>
> *Biblical truth: Faith is a calm assurance that the object of my faith will respond according to its nature. True faith develops from a catalog of experiences of the faithfulness of the object of my faith.*

I Have No Faith

I was visiting a Christian friend whom I'll call Emilia. Emilia had a health issue. When I offered to pray for her, she replied, "But I have no faith." Emilia's response reveals a common misunderstanding about faith for healing. We think we must psych ourselves up to believe that we will be healed. If we can't muster up enough faith, then the prayer won't work. Such an attitude leaves us feeling frustrated and defeated. We try to muster up our faith. We pray. We don't see the results that we expect. And then we become even more discouraged than when we started. We'll return to Emilia at the end of this chapter, but first we need to look at what true faith is.

What Faith Is Not

Jesus made it clear that faith is important in healing (Matthew 9:28–29; Mark 9:22–24; Luke 8:48–50). But what does it mean to have faith? How do we get the kind of faith that results in healing? Before we answer that question, let's look at what faith is not.

Faith Is Not a "Hail Mary"

I grew up in East Africa. There, football was something you played with your feet, using a round ball. When I was eleven, our family temporarily moved to Saskatchewan, Canada. Back in Canada, football was a game you played mostly with your hands, using an oblong ball. At school, during recess, we played tag football.

For those not familiar with the game, the offensive side has four opportunities, called downs, to advance the ball by ten yards. If we succeeded in advancing ten yards, we got four more downs. Before each down, the team huddled and planned the next play. Our options typically consisted of pass, quarterback sneak, handoff, or punt. If it was the fourth down and we needed a lot of yardage to get to first down again, we would huddle together and someone would say, "Let's do a Hail Mary." It took a while for this kid from Africa to learn that a Hail Mary was a play in which we had little chance of succeeding—usually a long pass—covered by a plea to Mother Mary for success.

This is many people's approach to faith. They don't expect to succeed in what they are attempting, but they throw in a little prayer in the faint hope of a positive result. This isn't faith; it's wishful thinking. Wishful thinking does not result in many people receiving healing.

Faith is not trying to muster up belief for an answer. Faith is not just hoping for a good result. So, what is faith?

What Faith Is

We see two main uses of the word "faith" in the Bible. When the Bible speaks of "the faith," it is speaking of the body of doctrine and practice passed on from the apostles. We see this usage in Acts 6:7, where it says, "The number of disciples in Jerusalem increased rapidly, and a large number of priests became obedient to the faith."[1]

The other way "faith" is used in the Bible carries the meaning of "trust, firm persuasion, confidence."[2] When God is the object of our faith, this is the kind of faith that brings healing and causes miracles to happen. We'll look at some biblical examples of this below, but first an illustration.

Faith Is Sitting in a Chair

This morning, I arrived at my office and sat on my chair. Then I walked around a bit, chatted with a colleague, and sat on my chair again. Later, I went to a photocopy shop and sat on a plastic stool while a computer operator printed and laminated my documents. Then I came back to my office and sat on my chair again. Each time I sat, I did so with a great deal of confidence. I entertained not a shred of anxiety that the chair would not support my weight. Not once did I close my eyes and try to muster up faith that the chair would hold me.

Why not? Because after hundreds of thousands of experiences over several decades, I can only point to one or two times in my life where a chair I attempted to sit on did not bear my weight. I have a calm assurance that chairs of all types will hold me.

---

1. For a very short list of other occurrences of the same meaning, see Acts 13:8; Romans 4:12; 1 Corinthians 16:13; Galatians 1:23; 1 Timothy 6:21.

2. *Mickelson's*, s.v. "G4102 pistis." The majority of the occurrences of the word "faith" in the Gospels have this meaning. In Matthew 21:21, this meaning of the word is paired with its opposite: doubt.

So what is faith? In simple language, faith is a calm assurance that the object of my faith will respond according to its nature.

How did I attain such a well-developed faith that chairs of all types will hold me? Did I strive to build up this faith? Did I psych myself up to believe that the chair would hold me every time I sat? No. This faith grew from a long history of personal experiences. I have a large catalog of faith-in-chair stories. True faith develops from a catalog of experiences of the faithfulness of the object of my faith.

If I sat on a chair and it collapsed under my weight, then my reaction would be shock and surprise. *Why did that happen? I have sat on chairs like this thousands of times before. Why didn't it work this time? What went wrong?* Likewise, if we have faith in God for healing and the person we pray for is not healed, then our reaction is shock and surprise. What went wrong this time?

Moses Had a Catalog of Personal Experiences

Moses and Aaron stood in front of a rock. They said to the people of Israel assembled before them, "'Listen, you rebels, must we bring you water out of this rock?' Then Moses raised his arm and struck the rock twice with his staff. Water gushed out, and the community and their livestock drank" (Numbers 20:10b–11).

How did Moses come to have faith that when he stretched out his staff, miraculous things would happen? It came from a catalog of experiences. These experiences began many years earlier in the desert of Midian. There, God told him to throw down his staff. It became a snake. He picked it up by the tail, and it became a staff again (Exodus 4:2–5). Moses stretched his staff over the Nile River and made the waters of Egypt undrinkable (Exodus 7:19–21). He brought four other plagues on the Egyptians by stretching out his staff. When Moses stood on the banks of the Red Sea and stretched out his staff, the waters parted (Exodus 14:16). He stretched out his hand again and the waters washed over the pursuing Egyptian army (Exodus 14:26–28). He struck a rock and water came out (Exodus 17:5–6). This catalog of experiences gave Moses strong faith that when he stretched out his staff, miracles would happen.

How to Grow in Faith

If faith naturally develops from a catalog of experiences, then the key to growing in faith is building up a lot of experiences. If you want to have strong faith that when you pray, people will be healed, then you need to be involved in a lot of prayers where people get healed. If you want that, you will need to pray for a lot of people. Here are four ways you can grow in faith.

1. Build Up Your Catalog of Experiences in a Safe Learning Environment

Not all environments are great for learning. Environments where there is fear of failure or pressure to perform are usually not good learning environments. Environments where there are skilled and loving teachers, many opportunities to practice, lots of encouragement, and no shame or penalty for failure are great places to learn.

A Great Learning Environment

I was on home assignment from our ministry in Bangladesh, attending an adult Sunday School class at our home church. The pastor was teaching us how to listen to God. After the teaching segment, we were divided into groups of two and told to ask God for a word for the person we were paired with. When I saw that I was paired with Dylan, I was immediately disappointed. I didn't think Dylan was as spiritually in tune with God as I was and I didn't expect him to receive a meaningful word for me. Dylan, full of self-doubt, didn't think God would give him a word for me either. After mumbling for a while that this wouldn't work and that God wouldn't speak to him, he opened his mouth and said, "Neil, God wants you to go back to Bangladesh." What Dylan didn't know was that for weeks I had been secretly wishing that God would change my assignment. Ministry in Bangladesh was tough, and I was hoping that God would tell me to do something easier. Instead, God spoke through Dylan and confirmed my calling.

What enabled Dylan to receive a word from God for me and then overcome his doubts and share it? The environment of safety in the room was the key. This was an ideal learning environment. There was a skilled teacher. There was safety. There would have been gentle correction if anyone made a mistake. And there was freedom to make mistakes without feeling shame. Unfortunately, this type of environment is rare.

A Not-So-Great Learning Environment

I heard about a ministry where people prayed for the sick. I already had some experience praying for the sick, but I was looking for more and to learn from people who were more advanced than I. I contacted this group and was permitted to visit. I felt like I was only very reluctantly admitted, and then only as an observer. It was several weeks before I was even allowed to pray for a sick person. This was not a great learning environment because of the barriers to entry. It seemed that one had to be at some great spiritual height simply to join the team. I was not encouraged to try, to fail, and to try again. The right environment not only makes it safe to fail without shame, but it encourages someone to try.

2. Build Up Your Catalog of Experiences by Hanging Around People of Faith

If you don't have the privilege of attending a class that provides a safe learning environment, there is another way to grow in faith. You can hang around people who have faith.

I Don't Have Faith for Eyes

I was sitting at the table in the dining area of the hotel where our organization was holding a conference. A friend was with me, and we were there to pray for people who had physical ailments. Rashid came for prayer, along with his wife. After they sat down at the table with us, Rashid described some sort of mucus problem in his left eye. I started by anointing him with a dab of oil on his forehead and praying for him. There was little or no change in his condition. I thought to myself, *I have faith for backs and musculoskeletal issues, but not for eyes.*

Then my friend prayed for him. He stood and slabbed a copious amount of oil on his palms, covered Rashid's eyes with his anointed hands, and prayed a bold, faith-filled prayer for healing. After the prayer, Rashid's eye problem was completely gone. Rashid's wife was so encouraged that tears of joy came to her eyes.

Seeing this healing, I was emboldened. I thought to myself, *I can do this too.* My catalog of experiences grew simply by watching someone else receive healing.

3. Build Up Your Catalog of Experiences by Taking Small Risks

When we desire to increase our physical fitness, we push ourselves to do things we haven't been doing. We must start if we haven't been doing any exercise at all. Or if we have been, we must increase our level of exertion. If we limit ourselves to only doing the activities we have been doing, we will never develop.

Similarly, building up a catalog of faith experiences requires us to push ourselves a little. Faith needs to be stretched, it needs to be used, if it is to grow. This stretching involves taking small risks. If we only do what we are comfortable with, we will not grow.

With exercise, we must be careful not to try to do too much on the first day of a new exercise program. If we do, we risk injury. Or we will feel so sore that we won't want to exercise again. We need to push ourselves a little, but not too much.

Likewise, we may injure our faith if we try to take too big a step before we are ready for it.[3] We do need to push ourselves to do things we haven't done before, but we can make mistakes if we try to take too big a step all at once. For many of us, simply asking to pray for someone is an appropriate step of faith, regardless of the outcome. All we are looking for here are little steps. At this stage, we are not concerning ourselves with the result, we are just taking a step.

Jumping into a Swimming Pool

I watched as the father stood in the chest-deep water and his child stood on the edge of the swimming pool. The father told his son to jump. And he did. The father caught him. They both laughed. Then the father helped the boy to the edge, where he repeated his act of courage. The boy seemed to never tire of jumping into his father's arms. He was building a catalog of experiences.

The boy was trying something in a safe environment that only had a tiny bit of risk. But I have seen other children standing at the edge of a pool, too scared to jump into the arms of their disappointed parent. The children who took the risk and jumped built up a catalog of experiences of their parent's faithfulness. The children who didn't continued to live in fear.

4. Borrow from Other People's Catalogs of Experiences

If I weighed three hundred pounds and had several experiences of chairs collapsing under my weight, my faith in chairs would not be quite so strong. I might walk into a room, look at the spindly chair placed before me and think to myself, *No way. I ain't sitting on that.* Now suppose the engineer responsible for the chair's manufacture assured me that he had personally tested the design of that chair up to five hundred pounds. Then choosing to sit on the chair might still be a matter of courage, but, more than that, it would be a matter of choosing to trust the words of a witness.

---

3. Romans 12:6 cautions us to use our gifts in proportion to our faith.

We have trustworthy witnesses in the Bible. We have trustworthy witnesses in modern-day accounts of healing.[4] We can add stories to our catalog of faith by believing the experiences of others, by believing trustworthy witnesses.

Crossing a Rickety Bridge

I was relatively new in Bangladesh and was still working on developing my language skills. This meant I had to spend time with people, going where they took me, eating what they gave me, and talking about what they wanted to talk about. One young man took it upon himself to show me around Kushtia, the town where I lived at the time. Since I had a motorcycle, he would sit on the back behind me and tell me where to go. I learned that one way to cross a river was to drive my motorcycle onto a little boat. Most boats had a split bamboo floor almost as high as the lip of the boat. I would drive from the dock right onto the boat. The front wheel of my motorcycle practically hung over one side of the boat, while the rear wheel touched the other side. As the boatman crossed, I straddled the motorcycle with my feet on the bamboo floor to keep it upright. Then when we got to the other side, I drove off.

One day my friend took me to a ravine spanned by a narrow bridge. The bridge was probably only four feet wide. There was no railing on the bridge and several of the bridge's wooden planks were missing. My friend instructed me to drive over the bridge. I hesitated. In fact, I parked my motorcycle on the side of the path so I could have time to think about it. I expressed my doubts that the bridge would support the weight of me and my motorcycle. My friend insisted that the bridge was safe and would certainly hold our weight.

Another man walked up. He corroborated my friend's testimony: the bridge would support the weight of a motorcycle. I still sat stuck in indecision. As I weighed the pros and cons, a motorcyclist came up and confidently drove across.

---

4. If you are looking for a meticulously researched catalog of modern-day miracles, complete with a thorough examination of the evidence, then see Craig S. Keener's two-volume *Miracles*. For a shorter book written for a popular audience, see Keener's *Miracles Today*.

"See," my friend said, "I told you that motorcyclists use this bridge all the time." I was still undecided. *That motorcycle was smaller than mine. Maybe the bridge can support smaller motorcycles, but not heavier ones like mine.*

I debated for a long time, and ultimately chose not to take the risk. To my friend's disappointment, we took the long way around. I had an opportunity to exercise faith. I could have chosen to believe the testimony of my friend. Indeed, I could have chosen to believe what I had seen with my very own eyes: the bridge supported the weight of a motorcycle. But I never took that step of faith. I didn't have the courage to take that risk. I never drove across the bridge. By doubting the testimony of others, and even what I had seen with my own eyes, I did not add to my catalog of experiences. To this day I do not have confidence that the bridge will hold me.

Admittedly, there was a level of danger. If the bridge collapsed or I fell off, I would be stuck with a damaged motorcycle in a deep ravine, and perhaps with several broken bones. Likewise, praying for a sick person involves some risk, but the injury is only to our pride. If we want to grow in faith, we must learn to take small risks.

Coming Back to Emilia

When Emilia said, "I have no faith," I told her not to worry about her faith. I would pray using my faith. Since Emilia had several medical issues, I asked her to choose one that she wanted me to pray for. I generally find that trying to deal with every ailment all in one go is not helpful. Rather, it is better to choose one, pray for it, and then check in with the patient to see how she is doing. If the first issue is dealt with, then we can move on to the next. She chose one issue. I rebuked the problem and then invited her to do something she couldn't have done before without causing that issue to flare up. With courage she did so and did not experience the negative symptoms she would normally have experienced. Emelia experienced healing.

Start Praying for People

Faith is the natural by-product of a catalog of experiences with our faithful God. But what if you don't have that catalog of experiences? Then you need to listen to the words of a trustworthy source—the Bible, which demonstrates how Jesus longs to heal—and start taking some courageous steps. It is easier than we think, but what holds us back is our fear of falling. If you step out and it doesn't work, you don't risk a damaged motorcycle and broken bones. The only thing you risk is a slight bruise to your pride.

When I pray for someone, I rarely have faith that the person will be totally and instantaneously healed, although that sometimes does happen. Rather, I have the calm assurance that God is going to show up and something is going to happen in the life of the person I am praying for. That is all the faith I need to start praying.

Practically speaking, the best way to build your faith for healing is to start praying for people. Start building up a catalog of experiences. Ask what their symptoms are before you pray. Find out how they are feeling after you pray. Rejoice in the smallest sign of improvement. Eventually, you will find that someone gets healed. As you start praying for healing, your faith will begin to grow. I am certain that if you pray for one hundred people for healing based on the principles I've shared so far in this book, you will have more faith at the end of that time than when you started.

Conclusion

Faith is not psyching ourselves up to believe something. Faith is a calm assurance that the object of our faith will respond according to its nature. True faith develops from a catalog of experiences of the faithfulness of the object of our faith. The way to grow our faith is to build up this catalog of experiences. Ideally, some of these will take place in a safe learning environment where simply trying is celebrated and there is no penalty for failure. We can also build up our catalog of experiences by hanging out with a person of faith as they pray for the sick. Finally, we can build up our catalog by exposing ourselves to trustworthy testimonies.

Pray for one hundred people and see if your faith for healing is the same as when you started. If there is no change, I will gladly refund the price of this book.

Key Bible Passage

In the passage below, the apostles desire greater faith. Jesus simply tells them that a little faith can accomplish great things. Their task is to use the faith they have.

> The apostles said to the Lord, "Increase our faith!"
>
> He replied, "If you have faith as small as a mustard seed, you can say to this mulberry tree, 'Be uprooted and planted in the sea,' and it will obey you." (Luke 17:5–6)

Teaser

Are demons real? Can they affect Christians? In the next chapter, we will examine the relationship between demons and sickness.

Closing Prayer

Lord, faith is so deeply related to courage. We are afraid to pray because we are afraid that nothing will happen. We are afraid of what the person we are praying for will think of us if nothing happens. Sometimes we are even afraid of what people will think of you. Lord, help us to remember that you are big enough to take care of your own reputation. Our task is simply to step out in obedience and pray for people. Lord, help us to start taking some little steps of faith. Help us to take those little steps frequently.

Chapter Ten

The Demonic Aspect of Sickness

Demons Are Real and Sometimes Make Us Sick

> *Wrong belief: If demons are present today, they cannot cause serious problems in Christians. The demonic and sickness are unrelated.*
>
> *Biblical truth: Demons are present today and frequently cause sickness.*

Is the Devil Only a Concept?

A counselor and her husband were having dinner with us. Since I was curious about the impact of negative childhood experiences on adult behavior, I peppered her with questions. As we talked, I was taken aback by one comment. She said that Satan was a concept used to embody the evil in the world. Her conversation indicated that she did not believe in a real being called Satan or evil spirits under his power. My own experience, however, indicates the opposite. If we are going to be involved in ministering healing to others, we will encounter the demonic, just as Jesus and his disciples did.

A Demon in the Slum

A colleague and I had started a prayer ministry just inside a slum in Dhaka. This camp, a square block about two hundred meters on a side, was reported to be home to forty thousand people. Every Tuesday, we went to pray for the sick among the handful of believers in Jesus and some of their unbelieving friends. One day, a believing woman brought her niece, Janna, for prayer. Janna was dressed very nicely, with an elaborate Islamic hijab[1] covering her hair.

Janna told us her story. On the previous Thursday night, she had woken up to see three apparitions just outside her room. One was an old man with a broken arm, another had a broken leg, and the third was missing both eyes. Janna was terrified. She was certain this had not been a dream. Now, three days later, she was too scared to close her eyes and had barely slept since the event. She had been taken to a local Muslim healer, who gave her special holy water to drink. She was also given an amulet to wear. These cures had not helped, and Janna was still afraid to close her eyes.

My colleague and I were eager to pray, but we still had much to learn. My colleague ministered first. She asked Janna to close her eyes and tell us what she saw. Janna reported that one spirit came and pulled her hair, another pulled at her liver, and another pulled at another part of her body. My colleague then put her arms around her and prayed. I kept my eyes open and could see that Janna was still afraid to close her eyes. I saw her wince. After prayer, there was no change.

I told Janna to look into my eyes. With my eyes wide open, I looked into Janna's eyes and rebuked the spirits which were present and commanded them to leave. Janna said she felt lighter and believed that the oppressing spirits had

---

1. A hijab is a head covering worn by Muslim women.

left. My colleague again asked her to close her eyes to check. Janna now did this without fear.

Demons are real and they were oppressing Janna. She was freed by prayer in Jesus' name. Although Janna had heard much of the Christian faith, she had not identified herself as a follower of Jesus. Can Christians be tormented by demons?

A Demon in the Church

About six months prior to this, my friend had invited me to attend a rural church. The church met in a corrugated tin building about twelve feet by twenty feet in size, located in a village in the western part of Bangladesh. My friend told me that the Holy Spirit was really working in this church.

I visited one week, and, as the invited speaker, brought the message. After the main part of the service was over, those who wanted prayer lined up in front of the pastor's adult daughter, Mona. The noise and commotion were more than what I was used to in a prayer time, but it seemed that people were helped by Mona's prayers.

Tamara, a slight teenage girl, was next in line for prayer. She had put her faith in Jesus and attended the church regularly with her mother. Her complaint was bad dreams. Almost immediately after Mona started to pray, Tamara was on the floor in an all-out demonic manifestation. Four people held her down as she flailed about. Mona and others commanded the spirit to leave. They called down fire on the spirit. The pastor's son played worship music on his phone. Each of these actions produced dramatic contortions in Tamara, but no deliverance. Mona continued to pray and Tamara continued to writhe. After a while, Mona told us, "This is a persistent demon."

After watching the struggle and noise from a distance, the Lord seemed to speak to my heart: *Neil, you could help by praying instead of just standing there.* I started to pray from my position on the outer edge of the commotion, quietly rebuking spirits of sexual impurity. Then the Lord told me to go right up to the girl and pray for her there. I protested inwardly. *Lord, it won't look very good when the foreign visitor prays and nothing happens.*

Out of obedience, not expectation that anything would happen, I went up to the girl, held my hand over her as the others had done, and prayed according to the thoughts that the Lord seemed to be putting into my heart. Speaking quietly in English so no one else could hear or understand, I again rebuked a spirit of sexual impurity.

This rebuke brought an instant end to the drama. Tamara relaxed, opened her eyes, and looked at me. She was then perfectly well and stood up. This display of power shocked me to the core of my being. I was so surprised, I almost couldn't believe what I had just seen. But those in attendance had observed, and the next person in the prayer line wanted to be prayed for by me.

Can Demons Indwell Christians?

This is a difficult subject and much theological ink has been spilled on the matter. In the section below, I present my understanding of what the Bible teaches and invite my readers to examine the passages quoted and grapple with the issue themselves.

Most Christians assume that since the Holy Spirit resides within a believer in Jesus, demons cannot also reside within the same person. We need to ask ourselves, however, whether the Bible teaches that demons cannot dwell within Christians. One passage that has been used to attempt to show that Christians cannot be indwelt by demons is this:

> For what do righteousness and wickedness have in common? Or what fellowship can light have with darkness? What harmony is there between Christ and Belial? Or what does a believer have in common with an unbeliever? What agreement is there between the temple of God and idols? For we are the temple of the living God. (2 Corinthians 6:14b–16a)

Since light and darkness cannot inhabit the same physical space, people assume, based on this passage, that demons and the Holy Spirit cannot dwell in the same person. If we read this passage in context, however, we see that Paul is urging his hearers not to "be yoked together with unbelievers" (2 Corinthians 6:14a). He is not saying it is physically impossible to be yoked with an unbeliever. Rather, he is arguing that it is inappropriate to do so because righteousness and wickedness have nothing in common; light and darkness do not fellowship together.

In v. 17, he urges his hearers to "come out from them and be separate," implying that the children of light had been fellowshipping with the children of darkness. This passage neither states nor implies that a Christian cannot be indwelt by a demon.

Other passages used to try to prove that demons cannot indwell Christians are the following:

> No, in all these things we are more than conquerors through him who loved us. (Romans 8:37)

> For he has rescued us from the dominion of darkness and brought us into the kingdom of the Son he loves, in whom we have redemption, the forgiveness of sins. (Colossians 1:13–14)

> I am writing to you, young men, because you have overcome the evil one. (1 John 2:13)

If we use these passages to say that true Christians can never be indwelt by demons, then we must also say that true Christians can never live in spiritual defeat and can never engage in an activity that is part of the dominion of darkness. Practically speaking, very few Christians would claim that they always walk in victory and triumph. There are many examples of people who have given their hearts to Jesus, yet still live in the darkness of habitual sins and addictions from which they have not found freedom.

Returning to 2 Corinthians 6:14–16, the claim that Jesus or the Holy Spirit (the assumed meaning of "light" in this passage) cannot spatially be in the same place with Satan or demons (the assumed meaning of "darkness" in this passage) does not have biblical support.

Satan was present with Jesus when Jesus was tempted. In fact, Satan caused Jesus to supernaturally move to the pinnacle of the temple (Matthew 4:5) and to a high mountain (Matthew 4:8). I do not know if Jesus was bodily transported to these places, or if he was transported in spirit through a visionary experience. Nevertheless, Jesus was transported by Satan, implying they were in close proximity to each other. The Gospels relate many accounts where Jesus, full of the Holy Spirit, was physically close to those who were tormented by demons.

In summary, the Bible does not teach that a Christian cannot be indwelt by a demon. An illustration may clarify what I am saying.

Cockroaches in the Palace

There was once a magnificent palace indwelt by a mighty king. The palace had over one thousand rooms, most of which were stunningly decorated in gold and expensive fabrics. The floors were covered in Persian carpets, the walls with famous paintings, and the ceilings with jeweled chandeliers. This palace also had guardrooms, boudoirs, bathrooms, kitchens, pantries, larders, and cellars.

To claim that because the indwelling king was so mighty, rats and cockroaches could never enter the cellar is unfounded. The presence or absence of unwanted vermin is related more to the diligence of the cleaning staff than the greatness of the king.

Likewise, the King of Glory comes to dwell in our hearts when we surrender our lives to him. However, when Jesus enters, he may find a palace in ruin and disarray. Over a period of months or years, as we surrender each room to him, he cleans and purifies it, driving out unwanted inhabitants.

A Church Secretary's Experience

My experience, and the experience of others, indicates that demons can indeed dwell within genuine Christians. Peter Horrobin relates this example:

> There was a time some years ago, when I was preaching in a fairly typical Anglican church. I was five minutes into my sermon and beginning to teach about the power of the name of Jesus over all the powers of darkness, when a lady stood up on her pew and started shouting at me, "Shut up! Shut up! Shut up!" The demons within her could not stand what was being said.
>
> She tried to tear a Bible into small pieces to throw at me, but then the Holy Spirit fell upon her and she, like the man in Capernaum, was thrown down to the floor and finished up lying between the pews with her head on a hassock before she was delivered of an evil spirit. That church has never been the same since!
>
> Later that day there was a somewhat challenging discussion in the church about whether or not Christians could have demons. In the middle of the debate this lady got up, came to the front, took over the microphone and ended the discussion with one of the most profoundly brief statements on the subject I have ever heard. "Now listen," she said, "I'm your church secretary. I've been born again five years, and I didn't think I had a demon, but I did. And now I don't, so there!" With that she returned to her seat and saved the whole meeting hours of fruitless theological discussion! Christians certainly can, and do, have demons.[2]

---

2. Horrobin, *Healing through Deliverance*, loc. 1534 of 11137, Kindle.

We will see the connection between demonic activity and sickness in the next section.

The Demonic Element to Sickness

Satan "comes only to steal and kill and destroy" (John 10:10). It is logical to understand that part of this destruction comes through sickness. Indeed, we see sickness associated with the presence of demons multiple times in Jesus' ministry. In Matthew 4:24, we see "demon-possessed" included in a list of ailments that Jesus healed. When Jesus commissioned his disciples, he sent them to "heal the sick" and "drive out demons" (Matthew 10:8). A likely inference from these references is that many diseases are caused by evil spirits.

Moving beyond inference, the Gospels give specific examples of diseases caused by demons. A mute man spoke after a demon was cast out (Matthew 9:32–33). In Matthew 12:22, Jesus healed a "demon-possessed man who was blind and mute." Jesus healed a boy suffering from seizures by driving out a demon (Matthew 17:14–18). A severe case of curvature of the spine was caused by an evil spirit (Luke 13:10–13, 16).

The Gospels make a strong connection between evil spirits and illness. I suspect that in some cases the demon causes the illness, while in others, the demon opportunistically takes advantage of the weakened emotional condition caused by the illness to invade and take up residence. Do all sicknesses have a demon associated with them? I doubt it. Nevertheless, we ought to be open to the possibility that there is a demonic element behind the illness of the person to whom we are seeking to minister healing.

If the sickness has an unknown cause, if it is generalized pain, if pain moves from one part of the body to another during prayer, then we must be alert to the possibility that the demonic is involved. The antidote is to rebuke the pain and evil spirits associated with it. The way to deal with a demon is through rebuke and command in the name of Jesus.

If I stood in front of a large rock and started rebuking it, onlookers would correctly assume I had a few loose screws in my head. Rocks do not have the ability to hear, much less to understand and obey. Rebuking only makes sense if there is a sentient being present to listen and respond to the rebuke. Jesus rebuked a fever and Peter's mother-in-law was instantly healed (Luke 4:39). Jesus' rebuke should make us ask ourselves whether there was a demonic presence behind the fever. The fact that Jesus rebuked a storm prior to encountering a severely demonically afflicted man (Luke 8:22–27) makes us ask ourselves whether there was a demonic presence behind the storm.

A Demon Preventing Healing

I was in the crowded kindergarten classroom mentioned in chapter 1 of this book. A woman was there with serious lower back pain from which she had suffered for ten years. She told me that she couldn't get up from a squatting position without putting her hands on a wall for support. She stood facing me as I prayed for her. I began to pray with my eyes open. As I prayed, I could see that she was going to fall over backward.[3] My first impression was, *Wow! Someone is falling under the influence of the Holy Spirit while I'm praying. That has never happened to me before.* I grabbed her shoulders to steady her, but she continued to fall. Another woman was standing behind her and laid her down gently on the concrete floor. As she went down, I saw grimaces on her face and concluded that it wasn't the Holy Spirit who was in operation here.

Now she was on the floor and I was standing over her, sandwiched between the kindergarten desks. I thought to myself, *If there is an evil spirit involved and she starts thrashing around against the desks, either she or I will end up in some serious pain.* So, not knowing what else to do, I started rebuking all the different types of evil spirits I could think of. When I mentioned "spirit of abuse," she experienced some measure of relief. We helped her into a sitting position on one of the kindergarten benches. She said that the pain was reduced but not gone and that it seemed to her something was preventing her from getting well.

---

3. I don't encourage people to fall over backward. In some cases, this practice is a socially induced phenomenon.

I told those present that she was right. I read Luke 13:10–12, which talks about a woman who had been crippled by a spirit for eighteen years. This time I put my hand on her back and prayed for her again. There were more grimaces, but the pain went away. I had her test it. She went into a squatting position and was able to get up without grabbing on to anything. Afterward she said she felt light—a typical response after a demon leaves.

Explaining the Return of Sickness

I have prayed for many people and seen a dramatic improvement in their condition, or even total healing, only to see the sickness quickly return. Understanding the demonic aspect of sickness may help to explain this phenomenon.

Back Pain Returns

My colleague Lakshan came to the office one day in February wearing a back brace. He had spent several days lying flat in bed due to back pain. The pain had subsided somewhat and now he was up and about, but still in pain. I offered to pray for him. I began by asking a few questions about his condition. He rated his pain at three or four out of ten, but certain movements would cause the pain to spike back up to ten out of ten.

I invited Lakshan to take his back brace off, if he felt comfortable doing so. After he had removed it, I put my hand on his back and prayed for him and rebuked the pain. He said he felt a little better. I had him move around to check things out. He moved backward and side to side, and things seemed ok. Then he bent forward and was hit with a spasm of pain, spiking his pain score way up again.

This was a bit disappointing, and with considerably less faith than I had begun, I decided to give it another shot. The second time, I put my hand on his lower back in the place where I thought the tense muscles were. I rebuked the inflammation in the spaces between the vertebrae and commanded the inflammation to leave. He said, "That did it." This time he demonstrated complete healing. He bent down and almost touched the floor. Then he went down into a squatting position and got up unaided and without pain—activities he couldn't have done at all prior to prayer. He gratefully shook my hand to thank me.

After lunch, I was busy with a meeting. After the meeting, I was disappointed to learn that Lakshan's pain had returned. It was so bad that he left his motorcycle at the office and went home in an Uber. What explains the dramatic healing and equally dramatic return of the problem? One possibility is that Lakshan's pain was caused by an evil spirit. The evil spirit left at my rebuke, but Lakshan's doubt that he could be healed so quickly opened the door for the spirit, causing the pain to return.

Conclusion

Demons are present in the world today. They can wreak havoc in the lives of both Christians and non-Christians. Subservient to their master, Satan, their goal is to steal and kill and destroy. Causing sickness and preventing healing fall within their territory. The biblical record is clear that some sicknesses are caused by demons. Rebuke of the illness, and by extension, of any demons behind the illness, is an important part of healing methodology. The return of an illness may be an indicator that demons are at work.

I have come to some controversial conclusions in this chapter. If you cannot accept everything I have written, that is OK. It is enough to understand that demons can oppose Christians to various degrees and demons sometimes cause sickness.

Key Bible Passages

> Jesus left the synagogue and went to the home of Simon. Now Simon's mother-in-law was suffering from a high fever, and they asked Jesus to help her. So he bent over her and rebuked the fever, and it left her. She got up at once and began to wait on

them. (Luke 4:38–39)

The Lord answered him, "You hypocrites! Doesn't each of you on the Sabbath untie your ox or donkey from the stall and lead it out to give it water? Then should not this woman, a daughter of Abraham, whom Satan has kept bound for eighteen long years, be set free on the Sabbath day from what bound her?" (Luke 13:15–16)

When evening came, many who were demon-possessed were brought to him, and he drove out the spirits with a word and healed all the sick. (Matthew 8:16)

Teaser

In the next chapter we look at a practical how-to method for healing the sick.

Closing Prayer

Lord Jesus, I praise you for your victory over Satan and all his demons at the cross. Thank you for your shed blood, which not only cleanses us from sin, but also disarms the demonic powers and authorities. Help us to walk in victory over the powers of darkness.

Chapter Eleven

Training Wheels for Those Stepping Out in Healing

A Simple Step-By-Step Method

> *Wrong belief: When ministering healing, we must maintain an aura of success.*
>
> *Biblical truth: We should approach healing with honesty and love for the person to whom we are ministering. Healing is about bringing God's presence into the situation.*

How Not to Heal the Sick

The service was over at the little church we had been attending for the past six months. The pastor brought a woman to me and said that we were going to pray for her. She had several fatty lumps on her arms, likely a case of lipoma, a type of noncancerous tumor. The one on her right wrist was bothering her and she was scheduled to have an operation to remove it. Like many Bangladeshis, she was afraid of operations, and so was hoping that the tumor would disappear in answer to prayer. The pastor asked me to begin the prayer time.

I found the situation awkward for several reasons. We were all standing, rather than sitting together in a relaxed environment. I hadn't had a chance to interview the patient. There were several onlookers present. The noise and pressure of the situation did not make it easy for me to stop and ask the Lord what he wanted to do in this case.

I started to pray under my breath, asking the Lord how he wanted me to minister to the woman standing in front of me. I didn't get far. The pastor, not satisfied with my delay, burst in with his own prayer. His prayer consisted of a loud and long string of commands to be healed and rebukes of the ailment. After the prayer, the woman's husband—one of the onlookers—said that the lump had decreased. The pastor, seeing this as an indication that healing had begun, launched into another prayer for further healing. After the second prayer, the husband asserted that the lump had decreased even more. As a close onlooker, however, I had not observed any change. Shortly after, the family left, with the husband saying that the lump would continue to decrease in size.

I hadn't seen any indication that healing had begun or that God had begun to move in power. I was left with a feeling of disappointment. Surely we could have ministered to this woman in a deeper way.

Although God is not limited in what he can do, and he is certainly not limited by our bumbling and immature attempts to bring healing, there are several ways that this prayer time could have been made more effective.

Love the Whole Person

Before we start, we must make sure that our focus is in the right place. Our focus must be on loving the person in front of us (1 Cor. 13:1–2). Love is never about getting a healing that we can chalk up as our own success. Love requires time and a listening ear. Love means caring for the whole person, not simply focusing on the alleviation of symptoms. It would have been better to sit together before we began, and to ask a few questions. What were her fears? Why was she worried about the operation? How did she feel about herself? Did she think this disease was a punishment for something she had done? Had she tried any ungodly remedies?

Take Away the Pressure to Succeed

We need to create an environment that encourages total honesty. While there is a place for public healing ministry, that type of ministry is best done by people with many years of experience and a life characterized by an acute sensitivity to the voice of God. Praying in front of a curious crowd makes it difficult to fail gracefully. That in turn creates pressure in both the person praying and the patient to report healing when none has occurred. This type of situation can result in propagating a lie, whether intentionally or not—saying that healing has occurred when it hasn't. Asserting that a healing has occurred when there is no evidence to back it up may indicate a lack of honesty, not great faith. We must remove the pressure to succeed.

Allow for a Gracious Exit

As we will see in the next chapter, not everyone is healed when we pray. It may have taken a good deal of courage for the patient to even come forward and ask for prayer. When healing does not occur, both the person praying and the person being prayed for need to have a way to exit graciously. If lack of healing is attributed to a lack of faith on either the part of the patient or the part of the person praying, then there is no way to stop praying without admitting defeat or feeling like a failure.

Now, let's look at a better model.

Take Your Hand off—It's Too Hot!

In May 2020, Bangladesh was in lockdown. The house church that I was a part of had shifted to meeting online. During the online service one week, Payel requested prayer for severe back pain. After the service, I messaged her on WhatsApp and asked if she would like me to pray for her. When she assented, I video-called her.

When I called her, I saw her sitting next to her husband, Sagar. We talked about her back pain for a bit. The pain had started the previous afternoon. She had expected the pain to go away in the night, but it had not. Since Sagar was present, I asked him to put his hand on her back in the spot where the pain was while I prayed. I prayed and rebuked the pain. After the prayer, I saw Payel take Sagar's hand in hers and feel it. She had felt hot pressure on her back and assumed it was because Sagar's hand was unusually warm and that he was pressing on her back. But when she felt his hand, it was a normal temperature. Sagar said he had not been pressing and he had not sensed anything unusual.

After the first prayer, Payel's assessment was that her pain level had decreased from 9.5 out of 10 to 4.5 out of 10. I had felt God's presence during the first prayer and felt that we should have just sat in the Lord's presence for a few more moments. I prayed again. This time Payel felt muscle cramping in her back during the prayer and began to sweat. Now she said the pain was 3 out of 10. I prayed again, with more authority this time, and rebuked the spirits of pain. I also prayed for angels to be in their room and to keep any evil presence out.

Payel said that she felt how someone feels after they take acetaminophen for a fever and the fever breaks. "That is how I feel now. I am sweating." Sagar's hand was so hot, she told him to take it off. I told Sagar to put his hand back on anyway and to just wait. After waiting a while, Payel said the pain was very little, now 2 out of 10. She felt the pain would go away on its own. I, however, wanted the pain to go away completely right then, so prayed again. During this prayer, I heard the Lord telling me in my heart that the pain would go away over time. There was no change after this prayer. About two and half hours later, Payel texted the house church WhatsApp group with this message:

As I said, I was suffering from back pain. The pain was severe, and I was unable to do normal activities. In today's meeting, everyone prayed for me. Later, Uncle Neil personally prayed for me. During his prayers, Sagar put his hand on me as Uncle Neil was on the phone. Sagar's hand was getting too hot to tolerate. It felt like I was getting the hot water bag treatment. Then I heard the LORD'S voice. My pain is gone now totally. Praise the LORD.

Some Simple Steps

When we observe Jesus ministering healing, we see a vast variety in the ways he did it. He almost never did the same thing twice. We, therefore, cannot reduce ministering healing to a formula. Below I give some steps I use when ministering to others. Rather than seeing these steps as a formula, view them as training wheels on a child's bicycle. When the child becomes proficient at cycling, the training wheels come off.

Step 1: Preparation

The purpose of this step is to create an environment of relaxed anticipation. Both the patient and the person praying should be at ease. I like to begin by making the patient feel comfortable. I prefer to be seated and to have the patient seated also. Generally, I begin by asking about the nature of the condition, and how long the person has been troubled by it. While I am listening to the patient, I am also trying to listen to the Lord to see what he wants to do in the situation. What is his priority? What does he want to accomplish?

Although God desires our healing, it may be that there are other things he wants to do first. The best thing to do is to ask him and listen to the thoughts that he gives in our hearts in response to our questions. Sometimes God desires to deal with a heart issue before dealing with a physical issue. If there were traumatic events associated with the start of the pain, the Lord may want to deal with the trauma.

I want the patient to relax. I don't want her to feel that she must work up a certain amount of faith. Sometimes I say, "I don't know what will happen when I pray." I don't want to put pressure on either myself or the patient to make a certain result happen. If she says, "I don't have faith," then I tell her that I will pray using my faith.

If the issue is physically painful, I ask if the person is feeling pain right now, and if so, what the level of the pain is on a scale of one to ten. This is a subjective measurement, but it performs several important functions. First, it prepares both the patient and person praying to expect healing. Second, it helps the patient to notice small changes. For example, the patient's headache might not completely disappear, but it might begin to decrease. This is an indication that healing has started. Third, it helps the person praying know how to proceed.

Step 2: Prayer

Then I begin to pray. At this stage I am not praying for the patient as much as I am praying for myself. Sometimes I pray quietly to help my spirit tune in to what the Holy Spirit wants to do. I invite the power of God to come into the situation. An important component of healing is bringing the person into the presence of God.

If I don't yet have clarity on how to proceed, I need to stop and ask God what he wants to do. At times I even do this audibly. "Lord, I just want to stop for a moment and ask you what you want to do." I don't want to assume that God always works the same way in each situation.

Sometimes at this point I will stop my prayer and ask the patient more questions. Once I had started praying for a woman named Rina, who had back pain. During my prayer I remembered she was wearing an amulet. I stopped praying and asked if she would be willing to take the amulet off. She did so and put it on the dining table. I then rebuked the back pain and the pain decreased.

When I have a sense of what God wants me to do, I do it. There are many ways to minister healing. It could be through the laying on of hands, anointing with oil, commanding healing, or rebuking evil spirits that cause pain. In a learning situation, we often revert to doing all the above. That is not harmful, but it is better to slow down and listen to God. As we saw in chapter 7, in the Bible healing is effected through commands, not through petitions to God to heal.

We don't need to be in a hurry when ministering healing to a person. As we saw with Payel above, sometimes the power of God is a bit like a hot pack that you put on a sore muscle.

Step 3: Check-In

After the first prayer, I check in with the patient to see how she is doing. Here I want an honest answer. Does she feel better? Worse? The same? How does she feel emotionally? If the person has been suffering from a physically painful body part, I ask her to move around and check it out.

Tony's Vertigo

A new friend named Mario and I were praying for several men at a Christian campground in Ontario one morning in July. Tony had been in bed most of the previous day due to vertigo. After we prayed for him, Tony checked out whether the vertigo had gone or not. First, he shook his head violently from side to side—something he could not have done the previous day. Then he stood up and bent over double. He was amazed at the healing he'd experienced.

Step 4: Repeat If Necessary

If the patient has experienced healing, then rejoice. Sometimes the patient experiences healing but can hardly believe it. Our confirmation that the healing is real can strengthen their faith. If there is no visible healing, or if the healing is partial, we can ask for the opportunity to pray again. If each time we pray there is a little bit more healing, we can continue to pray. If after praying twice, there is no more change, that is often an indication that we should stop.

We must keep the patient's needs and well-being in mind at all times. If we keep praying when the patient would rather have us stop, then we are no longer loving the patient. Some people, eager to see God work, pray multiple times while the patient begins to feel more and more awkward. When healing does not come immediately, the patient might feel that there is something wrong with her. Or she might feel pressure to declare improvement when there is none. We must be sensitive to the needs of the individual over our desire to see healing.

Sometimes God has worked during the first prayer, but the effects of the healing come later. Patience and persistence are often required.

Pre-baptismal Healing

Chaya and Rema were talking together after church one day. Rema was a new believer and Chaya was going to baptize her that afternoon. Chaya saw me and started telling me about her leg pain. She asked me to pray for her. Aware of the problems that arise when new believers think that only the foreign worker can pray for healing, I encouraged Rema to put her hands on Chaya and pray.

After the first prayer, nothing happened. I encouraged Rema to try again. After the second prayer, there was some improvement. I told Rema to pray again. After the third prayer, Chaya declared with an oath that she was healed. I'm sure that was an encouragement for Rema on the day of her baptism.

Step 5: Post-Prayer Instructions

Finally, I stop and ask the Lord if he has any words to give to the patient. Sometimes it is helpful to warn that pain may seek to return. In this case, the remedy is for the patient herself to rebuke it.

Three Helpful Tips

Here are three things that I have found helpful as I seek to minister healing to people. First, start small. Rather than choosing as my first prayer subject someone who has terminal cancer, it is better to start with something smaller. What about the cure of a headache or a fever or a cold? As we start with smaller issues, our faith builds up to the place where we are ready to face larger challenges. Second, expect some change. We might not have faith for complete and instantaneous healing. But we can believe that God will show up and at least begin to heal. As we see something change in the person we are ministering to, our faith grows to expect more. Finally, we should be bold, not half-hearted, as we minister. The woman with the bleeding problem wasn't half-hearted in her pursuit of Jesus. Somehow, she pushed through the crowd and managed to touch Jesus' cloak (Mark 5:27–31). Similarly, Jesus taught that we should speak with "boldness" (NIV, 1984 version) or "shameless audacity" when we pray (Luke 11:8). This attitude of boldness applies when we rebuke sickness as well.

Conclusion

Praying for people is about loving God, loving the other person, and relaxing. Do your best to remove fear and pressure. You don't need to be in a hurry. Don't try to get the patient to force themselves to believe. The process will go much better if we take it easy and enjoy the time ministering rather than focusing on our own success.

When we are learning how to pray for healing, it helps to have a simple method to follow, like the one given in this chapter. After some experience, we can just listen to the Holy Spirit.

Key Bible Passage

As the following passage shows, on occasion, even Jesus had to minister more than once to bring full healing.

> They came to Bethsaida, and some people brought a blind man and begged Jesus to touch him. He took the blind man by the hand and led him outside the village. When he had spit on the man's eyes and put his hands on him, Jesus asked, "Do you see anything?"
>
> He looked up and said, "I see people; they look like trees walking around."
>
> Once more Jesus put his hands on the man's eyes. Then his eyes were opened, his sight was restored, and he saw everything clearly. (Mark 8:22–25)

Teaser

There are instances mentioned in the Bible, and we see the same in our real-life experience, when people receive prayer but are not healed. We will talk about what to do in this situation in the next chapter, and examine some reasons why people are not healed in the chapter after that.

Closing Prayer

Lord Jesus, I thank you that you are the healer. Thank you also that you want me to minister alongside you to a suffering world. Help me to ditch my fears, have fun, and bless and heal suffering people in your name.

Chapter Twelve

What About All Those Who Are Not Healed?

Responding with Love and Honesty When Sickness Remains

> Wrong belief: If I do everything right, everyone I pray for will be healed.
>
> Biblical truth: Apart from Jesus, there is no example of 100% success in healing ministry in the Bible. We, therefore, cannot expect 100% success when we pray for the sick.

Odessa's Objection

It was summer in Ontario, and my wife and I were sitting in the backyard of Odessa's house, having dinner. I was excitedly talking about the event described in chapter 1 where the Lord led me to invite someone from the audience to come forward for prayer. I described how before I had even finished praying, the woman was healed. Odessa replied, "What about all those who are not healed?" The implication behind her comment was that those who talk about healing are disingenuous because they don't talk about their failures.

In one sense, she was right. Those who pray for healing don't often go around talking about the people who don't get healed. But then again, neither do evangelists talk about the people who didn't turn to Jesus, nor do pastors talk about the sermons that put their hearers to sleep. We talk about what is exciting to us. We talk about our victories.

Odessa was also correct that many people are not healed even after loving, faith-filled prayer. In my own experience, it is rare for someone to experience full and instantaneous healing after the first prayer. Many of those I pray for do not report healing at all. Nevertheless, more people have been healed in the three years since I began praying for the sick regularly than in my prior three decades of life and ministry.

People in the Bible Who Were Not Healed

The Bible mentions several people who were not healed, or at least not healed instantly.[1] Paul left Trophimus, one of his traveling companions on his third missionary journey, sick in the city of Miletus (2 Timothy 4:20). Epaphroditus also seems to have fallen seriously sick, sick to the point of death, when Paul was present or nearby (Philippians 2:27). Epaphroditus eventually recovered but this does not seem to be an example of an instantaneous recovery like those recorded elsewhere in the Bible.

Paul himself suffered an illness that resulted in him preaching the gospel to the Galatians (Galatians 4:13). Timothy, a disciple of Paul and one of his traveling companions, had longstanding digestive troubles. Paul told him, "Stop

---

1. Many of these examples were gleaned from Keener's *Miracles Today*, 224.

drinking only water, and use a little wine because of your stomach and your frequent illnesses" (1 Timothy 5:23).[2]

In the Old Testament, Elisha was known for great healing miracles, such as healing a town's water (2 Kings 2:21), raising a dead boy to life (2 Kings 4:32–37), healing Naaman the leper (2 Kings 5:1–14), and blinding and then restoring sight to an entire army (2 Kings 6:18–20). Yet Elisha himself eventually died of a sickness (2 Kings 13:14). And we cannot conclude that Elisha regressed spiritually in his old age and that is why he got sick and died. Even while he was sick, God's prophetic unction was upon him to such an extent that he accurately predicted the defeat of Aram (2 Kings 13:14–20). After his death, so much spiritual power surrounded his body that a recently deceased man came to life as soon as his body came into contact with the bones of Elisha (2 Kings 13:21).

If great men of God such as Elisha and Paul still experienced sickness, if men like Paul were not able to instantly heal all those around them, then it is natural to assume that we will not experience 100% success in healing either.[3]

Wrestling with Failure in Healing

Bible teacher and faith healer Andrew Wommack raised a dead person to life. Sometime later, he went to Nebraska, to speak at a meeting there. In the audience he saw a paralyzed man in a wheelchair. Remembering the recent resurrection, Wommack was confident that he had sufficient faith to heal a paralyzed

---

2. Prescribing wine for digestive troubles is not without medical foundation. It could be that mixing wine with water destroys sickness-inducing waterborne microbes. See Weisse, "Wine as a Digestive Aid," for the antibacterial properties of wine. It could also be that wine itself, in moderation, improves the health of the digestive tract (see Biasi, "Wine Consumption"). There is no indication in the Bible that Paul was opposed to the use of medicine for sickness.

3. I have heard testimonies of all the sick present at a single meeting being healed. Indeed, we see biblical examples of this occurring in Acts 5:16 and Acts 28:9. However, based on the examples listed above, I don't believe there is anyone who has not occasionally faced failure as they attempted to minister healing.

man. He reports, "I went over and grabbed this man by the hand and lifted him out of the wheelchair and he fell right over on his face." The crowd gasped and groaned as Wommack got the paralyzed man back into his wheelchair.[4] The man was not healed, and it must have taken a miracle for Wommack to finish his sermon.

Though perhaps not as dramatic as Wommack's experience, every person who ministers healing must deal with failure. David Edwin Harrell, in his masterful study of the charismatic revivals in America in modern times, writes:

> In the final analysis, the persistent, goading presence of failure was simply one of those paradoxes inherent in every theological system. Pentecostal historian John T. Nichol wrote: "One of the dilemmas that periodically confronts the Pentecostals is that some people who desire healing are not healed. A typical response to this seemingly incongruous situation is that a doctrine of divine healing in the work of the atonement must leave a place for permitted sickness as an expression of divine wisdom or divine purpose, inscrutable though it may be." Not until recent years have some of the more thoughtful charismatic evangelists honestly and openly confronted the problem of failure.[5]

Honest people in the healing ministry do not claim one hundred percent success. Yet, I believe we should seek healing until God clearly tells us that we

---

4. See Wommack, "The Problem Is Our Unbelief." This incident starts at minute thirty. I applaud Andrew Wommack for his integrity and willingness to share his failures publicly. Wommack's interpretation of this event is that he had faith, but he also had unbelief. "Sometimes your faith is not the problem, you just need to drain out your unbelief so that your faith can work."

5. Harrell, *All Things Are Possible*, 115. Also, Harrell recommends Oral Roberts' *The Call*, 1971, 45–56, as a thoughtful, honest, and open confrontation of the problem.

should no longer do so. Note, however, that praying and not seeing an answer must not be construed as hearing God's voice. Construing a failure in healing to be God's voice is equivalent to obtaining direction by relying on circumstances alone. God frequently asks us to fight against prevailing circumstances, not be led by them.

There are many reasons why our prayers for healing are not answered. God's unwillingness to heal is not usually one of them. Harrell suggests we should not simply attribute the lack of healing to the inscrutable will of God; rather, we should work through the subject more deeply. I attempt to do this in the following chapter.

Ken Blue, in his excellent book *Authority to Heal*, says:

> Sometimes the uneven quality of our healing ministry is starkly evident. A group of friends and I spent two hours praying over three people in wheel chairs one evening after a healing seminar. One of the three was a woman in the final stages of multiple sclerosis, another was a man with a spinal injury which left him paralyzed from the chest down, and the third was an ex-dancer who now could not even stand upright because of severe arthritis. We prayed with the same love and skill or lack of them for all three, yet at the end of two hours only one was up and walking—the lady with MS. She seemed to have no more faith than the others and claimed to be no more deserving; yet after two years in her chair she got up. Months later and still improving, she is now almost back to normal. The remaining two are grateful for the loving care they received then and since, but are only slightly improved physically.[6]

---

6. Blue, *Authority to Heal*, loc. 970 of 1544, Kindle.

If some people are healed when we pray and some people are not, despite the same levels of compassion and faith, maybe we ought not to put ourselves under undue pressure to obtain results. Perhaps we ought to content ourselves with obeying Christ's command to heal as best we can and not be overly troubled when we don't always see what we desire to see.

What Not to Do When the Person Is Not Healed

We were at a conference when I learned about Natalie's foot pain. The pain had started four and a half years ago. She thought the pain was due to walking in bad shoes she wore at the time. As I questioned her, she told me that it was not a particularly stressful time when the pain started, and the pain was not the result of an accident—answers which ruled out emotional trauma as a likely source. She said she had pain in both feet when she stands or walks for a long time. At times the pain reaches seven out of ten, but at the time we prayed, she wasn't feeling any pain.

I prayed for her. There was no sensation in her body. I put my hand on her feet and prayed again. Again, there was no sensation nor any indication of any form of healing. I began to feel a bit silly. Her husband suggested that the healing might come later. Later that day, they went for a walk. Then, in the late afternoon after they returned, I observed Natalie with her feet up over the arm of a chair, indicating to me that her feet were hurting. The next day she told me that her feet were worse than they had ever been.

Despite my prayers, Natalie wasn't healed. When we pray and there is no indication of any sort of healing, what should we do? What shouldn't we do?

Don't Become Upset

If we pray for someone's healing, and then due to lack of results we become upset, we reveal that something is wrong with our own hearts. If we get upset when someone is not healed, it can be an indication that our focus is more on ourselves than on the patient.

Don't Promise Healing Later

Don't give a false promise. Don't tell the person that they will recover unless you have very clearly heard the Lord tell you that they will recover. Don't declare that the person is healed when there is no change in the symptoms. It is possible that the healing process has begun, and the person will begin to feel better later, but it is equally possible that nothing has happened. Usually, if the healing has begun, you will see some indication of this during the prayer time.

Don't Blame the Patient for Lack of Faith

When we pray and there is no indication of healing, we may feel embarrassed. In that situation, it is tempting to deflect the blame for the lack of results to cover over our own shame. Such deflection is harmful.

One deflection strategy is to blame the patient for their lack of faith. Yes, faith is a factor, as we saw in chapter 9. But the faith of the healer, the patient, and the community all play a part. It could be that the person was not healed due to a lack of faith—a lack of your faith, not the lack of the faith of the patient. Although Jesus commended some people for their great faith, not everyone who was healed by him had faith for their healing. In the town of Nain, Jesus saw a dead person, the only son of a widow, being carried out for burial. The son was dead and could not be expected to have faith for his healing. There is no record that the widow had faith either. Yet Jesus raised the son to life (Luke 7:11–15).

At another, more well-known, resurrection, the climate also seems to have been a climate without faith. Dead Lazarus couldn't be expected to have faith. His sister Martha didn't want to open the tomb because of the stench of the decomposing body, indicating her lack of faith. Despite this lack, Jesus raised Lazarus to life (John 11:32–45).

In another situation, Peter and John healed a crippled beggar. The only thing that man had faith for was a handout, yet he was still healed (Acts 3:1–8).

Although lack of faith is not always a barrier, in some cases it is a barrier to healing (Mark 6:5–6). Yet blaming the patient for their lack of faith or exhorting them to have more is not likely to inspire true faith. Rather, if the patient is willing, a gentle exploration of why they do not have faith may be more helpful.

Don't Blame the Patient for Sin

There are no examples of Jesus rummaging in people's lives looking for sin before he healed them. As we saw in chapter 5, although sin may be a cause of sickness, sin is not necessarily a barrier to healing. Consequently, we should be extremely cautious about concluding that a sin may be preventing a healing. Yes, the patient may have sin in their life, but which of us can claim to be without sin? If a particular sin is preventing God's healing power from entering a person's life, then we can trust God to reveal this to us or to the person we are praying for. Yet we need to tread carefully, lest we accuse someone falsely.

What to Do Instead

There are several things we can do when a person we pray for is not healed.

Focus on the Patient, Not on Yourself

Get over your own awkwardness and focus on the patient. Being prayed for and expecting an immediate result may be way out of the patient's comfort zone. It may have taken a significant amount of courage on the patient's part to even to allow herself to be prayed for. She might already feel at fault for not being healed. Thank the person for coming. Congratulate her on her courage to seek healing and encourage her to keep seeking. Admit that you are still learning.

Offer to Pray Again Another Day, If Appropriate

Jordan Seng suggests:

If you pray for a person to get healed or delivered, and it doesn't work, what should you do then? You should be sensitive to the person's disappointment and as supportive as can be, but if at all possible you should also go get more power and try again. The key to supernatural ministry is to develop in power. It's helpful if everybody involved understands this so that we're free to respond to people's disappointments with repeated and increased efforts.[7]

Stay Curious

If we pray and there is no healing, we should stay curious. What is going on? What is God doing? Is there something he wants to say? Listening to the voice of the Holy Spirit is crucial. An unexpected lack of result is a great opportunity to learn. After every time we minister to someone, we have an opportunity to process the event with the Lord. This is the topic of the next section.

How to Process a Failed Healing

When we pray and the person is not healed, we tend to get discouraged. Rather than give up in despair, we should process what happened with the Lord.

Processing Nazrul's Lack of Healing

Nazrul came to me before the church service on Friday with bad neck pain. He said the pain level was eight out of ten. I prayed for him before the service to

---

7. Seng, *Miracle Work*, 74.

little or no effect. When I saw that there was no result, I offered to pray for him again after the service.

During the service, I wondered what was going on. My first thought was self-centered: *Am I losing my touch?* But as I continued to ponder the matter, I wondered if the Lord wanted someone else to pray for Nazrul.

After the service I found Nazrul talking with his friend Chanchal while waiting for me to pray for him. Since Chanchal was right there, I decided to test out my hypothesis. I gave Chanchal a bit of instruction and then told him to pray and then command healing. He did so. Nazrul said the pain was now five out of ten. I told Chanchal to pray again. Nazrul then reported that the pain was gone.

If I had not processed that failed healing with the Lord, I would have been left with a self-focused thought centering on my own failure. Instead, I asked Chanchal to pray, resulting in at least three people being encouraged: Nazrul, Chanchal, and me.

When processing a failed healing, good questions to ask are the following: *Lord, how did things go from your perspective? Did I respond to you correctly in offering to pray for that person? Did I pray for the right thing? Was there anything else you wanted to do that I missed? What is your view of me in light of this situation?* Ideally, you will write answers to these questions in a journal and then share them with a mentor.

Conclusion

If we step out in the healing ministry, we will encounter situations where the person we pray for is not healed or is not completely healed. I could fill a book with stories of people I have prayed for who were not healed. If we cannot "fail" graciously, then perhaps we should examine our own motives for praying for the sick. We should focus on obedience regardless of results and loving the person we are praying for.

Failed healings are not due to a problem or unwillingness on God's part. The lack is in us. Jesus is the only one with 100% success, but even he was hampered by lack of faith (Mark 6:4–6), and at times he had to minister more than once (Mark 8:22–25).

Key Bible Passages

> Stop drinking only water, and use a little wine because of your stomach and your frequent illnesses. (1 Timothy 5:23)

> Erastus stayed in Corinth, and I left Trophimus sick in Miletus. (2 Timothy 4:20)

Teaser

In the next chapter, we will delve into this topic more deeply and look at several reasons why healing does not occur.

Closing Prayer

Lord Jesus, healing is sometimes hard. Sometimes I get discouraged and want to quit. Help me not to quit, but to keep learning from you and growing in the area of ministering healing to others. Most of all, let me be full of love, regardless of the results I see.

Chapter Thirteen

Why Doesn't It Always Work?

Some Reasons Why People Are Not Instantly Healed

> *Wrong belief: If a person is not healed, then it simply wasn't God's will for the person to be healed.*
>
> *Biblical truth: There are many practical reasons why we do not effectively minister healing in a given situation.*

Back Pain That Didn't Leave

The day my prayer partners met together for lunch with their wives, Anne had been sick for the past month. That day, Anne's main complaint was a bad sore throat and fatigue. We gathered around to pray for her with the laying on of hands. With authority, I rebuked the sore throat. The throat pain left, and Anne didn't feel the need for me to pray for anything else. She was surprised that the pain had immediately gone away. When we parted, Ingrid, who herself had not been feeling well, hugged Anne and said, "It's OK if two sick people hug each other." Anne responded, "I feel really great now."

Two days later, our team met together at Edward's house for a prayer meeting. Over the past couple of weeks, Edward had been suffering through yet another episode of severe back pain. He was being treated three days a week at a physiotherapy clinic. Excited about all the healings I had recently seen, I offered to pray for Edward. I prayed for him with all the prayers I normally prayed, and nothing changed. After several minutes, we as a group prayed for him again and there was still no change.

Why was Anne healed but not Edward? In chapter 4, we saw how Jesus demonstrated God's will, and Jesus never turned a person away sick. Yet in our real-life experience not everyone we pray for is healed. How do we reconcile these two opposing concepts? In this chapter, I will give several reasons why people do not experience the healing that God is willing to give.

1. Lack of Experience

When we first begin praying for people, we can be quite nervous. We don't know exactly what to say to the patient. We don't know how to frame our prayer. We may not be adept at listening to God and tuning in to him while we are interacting with the patient. When we are distracted by our own nervousness, we don't remember to look to Jesus and believe that he is with us and wants to work. As a result, our prayers may not be effective in the beginning of our journey. After praying for people several times, tuning in to God while interacting with the patient in a relaxed and loving way becomes automatic.

2. Mental Blocks

I was on a Zoom call with several people. One of the participants, Chelsey, was sick. I asked her if she would like me to pray for her at the end of the call. She said, "That never works for me." But she allowed me to pray anyway. I prayed, but there was no immediate change in her situation. When a person goes into a time of prayer with the expectation that prayer will not work for her, the one praying must cross a big obstacle. There was a mental block on Chelsey's part which needed to be removed. Healing is a release of God's power into a situation. We can have attitudes and mental strongholds that block the flow of this power.

3. The Patient Is Not Ready

Sometimes the patient is not ready for prayer for physical healing. Emotional work needs to take place first. Jesus once asked an invalid, "Do you want to get well?" (John 5:6). The question makes us wonder if Jesus occasionally encountered people who did not want to get well.

Sometimes the lack of readiness stems from a sense of guilt. Although, as we have seen before, Jesus never made getting oneself spiritually cleaned up a prerequisite for healing, sometimes people view their sickness as divine retribution for past sins. If the patient believes he deserves to be sick because of sins he has committed, then prayers for healing are unlikely to work until the underlying guilt is removed.

4. Improper Method

If I randomly scatter some seeds on a patch of ground, some of them may grow. However, if I prepare the soil by digging it up, watering it, and spreading fertilizer, I will see more of my seeds sprout when I plant them.

God can and does work when our methods are flawed. However, employing the correct method will result in greater effectiveness. One problem is not using commands. We spend lots of time praying, even begging God to heal, but we don't do what we should be doing: commanding sickness to be gone, commanding the body to healed, and commanding evil spirits to leave. We beg God to do what he commanded us to do, and then are disappointed when he doesn't perform according to our expectations.

5. Insufficient Spiritual Power

Insufficient spiritual power is one of the greatest barriers to healing. I have referred to Jordan Seng previously in our study of power. I quote him again because he speaks to this issue in a most helpful way.

> I came to believe that if I failed at a healing or deliverance, it was probably because I was executing it incorrectly. But in reality, method is not nearly as important as power. It's not even close.
>
> Why do some people seem to get more results from, say, praying for healing than other people do? Why don't they always get good results? God's power is unchanging, but people's level of empowerment can vary a great deal.[1]

As we saw in chapter 8, we can grow in power. Time spent in personal (Mark 9:29) and corporate prayer (Acts 4:30–31) fervently asking God to release his power will result in greater power being demonstrated.

The power of Jesus' presence seems to be multiplied when people are gathered together in unity. It is my firm belief that if we had one hundred power-filled people joined together in heartfelt unity in prayer for a cancer patient, the results would be greater than if just one person prayed.

At the end of chapter 1, I wrote about a woman who was publicly healed at Elim Lodge. I had invited the audience to pray together with me and those present did so with sincerity. The woman was instantly healed.

---

1. Seng, *Miracle Work*, 54, 74.

6. Lack of Sensitivity and Obedience to the Holy Spirit

I was going to visit my friend Nasir. Before the visit, I asked the Lord if there was anything I should share with him. The answer I received was, "Ask him if he believes in God." In a culture where many educated, secular Muslims don't actually believe in God, this question could have generated some interesting conversation. When I got there, however, I didn't have the courage to ask that question. Instead, Nasir had a headache and I offered to pray for healing. He was not healed. This was a case of me not being responsive to what the Holy Spirit was inviting me to do in a particular situation.

The teenage son of our longtime Muslim friends had back pain. His father told me that the pain was caused by staying up all night in his chair playing video games. I talked with the boy about his chair, gave him a stretching exercise, and then asked if he wanted me to pray for him.

Before I prayed, I felt that God wanted me to talk to him about his video game usage. I thought to myself, *He will listen better if he is healed first.* Instead of responding to God's prompting, I went ahead and prayed for him. He did not feel anything and there was no improvement in his back. I prayed for him again and still there was no improvement. I was embarrassed. I wanted to demonstrate the power of God to this Muslim family. God wanted me to talk about video games.

We must learn to listen to what the Holy Spirit is saying. I cannot just expect to do a miracle if I don't pay attention to what God wants to do in the situation.

7. Quitting Too Soon

In January 2022, the omicron variant of COVID-19 was at its peak in Bangladesh. Almost everyone seemed to know someone who had either symptoms or positive COVID-19 test results. Foyez was sick, so I offered to pray for him over WhatsApp. Wrapped in a blanket, he did not look good on the video call that Tuesday morning. He had a deep chest cough and body pain. I prayed for him. I prayed that the fire of God would come. I cursed the virus. After the prayer, he got hot and removed the blanket. His headache decreased. Later in the day, though, he was still not feeling good. His headache returned in full force, he had eye pain, and was feeling terrible.

I called him again to pray for him that evening. Then he was very tired and had pain in all his joints. He still had a headache. After the first prayer, he said, "My body was very hot before. During the prayer it became pleasantly cool." I prayed again. Previously, his headache had felt like an electric shock to his head. This unpleasant sensation left.

The following two days, however, were difficult. By Thursday afternoon, he felt very weak and had pain breathing. On Friday, I called him again. He told me that he had wanted to study the Bible and as soon as he sat down, he felt uneasy. The restlessness started right after he joined the online Friday church service. He had wanted to bring the family together to pray, but couldn't. I suspected this was a demonic attack, taking advantage of Foyez's sickness.

I prayed, declaring Christ's victory, asking for God's light and angels to fill that room. Afterward he said, "I feel some peace now." He stretched his head back and forth several times and moved his shoulders. He said he got a cool feeling in his spine. He looked like he was feeling a bit better. Then he said, "I feel good, I feel refreshed. The uneasiness has gone." The following morning, I received this update: "I have just a little cough, but I feel completely well. Praise God."

A big issue is the time involved—sometimes we simply do not take the time required to minister healing in a loving and effective way. If the person is not healed after one or two prayers, we give up.

8. The Healing Has Started, But It Takes a While for the Symptoms to Change

Sometimes, the healing begins during the prayer, but it takes a while for the effects to be seen. At the end of the second day of a seminar one June, Mabruk wanted prayer for his prostate and other medical conditions. I was tired but prayed anyway. Two and a half months later, Mabruk called me one evening and reminded me of my prayers for him. He had received the results of a prostate examination that day and it was now normal size. He said that he still felt sick immediately after I prayed for him, but he slowly recovered. As he recovered, his prostate problems decreased.

9. Lack of Faith

Many times, our faith is at a low ebb. Sometimes we have faith for some ailments but not for others, because we have seen some ailments healed, but not others. Jesus can heal with little or no faith in either the patient or the person praying. However, commands for healing work better when the person praying and the patient both exercise faith.

I was feeling sick and miserable one day and asked my friend Jonathan to pray for me. Before his prayer, I apologized for my lack of faith. Jonathan kindly replied, "It is hard to have faith when you are sick." We should remember Jonathan's gracious words as we minister healing to others. It can be hard to exercise faith when one is sick, and harshly urging the patient to have faith usually does not help.

In certain situations, we need more than the faith of the person praying; we need an environment of faith. Perhaps this is why both Jesus and Peter removed those who did not have faith from the room when a resurrection was needed (Matthew 9:23–25; Acts 9:36–41).

In Troas one night, Paul spent a long time talking to the people. I'm sure he told how God had displayed his healing power during Paul's travels. When a miracle of resurrection was needed, the faith of the gathered community was already at a high level. Eutychus was raised from the dead (Acts 20:7–12).

10. End-of-Life Issue

Sometimes it is time to let our loved one go. Sometimes the sick person herself does not want to continue living. Mofazzel has been used by God to heal many people. He was once asked by a Christian family to pray for their elderly mother in the hospital. Mofazzel found the woman comatose and on life support. Mofazzel's only experience was praying for healing, so he prayed for her healing. Each time he prayed, the woman's body shook. After doing this three times, the family told him, "Actually, we want to release her." Mofazzel was taken aback. He had never prayed that someone would pass away before. Not sure if this was a correct approach to prayer, he prayed a prayer of relinquishment. The old woman died later that day.

None of us will live forever. There comes a time for each of us to pass away. When praying for people, especially those who are older, we can ask if God wants them to be healed, or if it is time for their earthly life to end.

11. Unknown Reason

We may do everything right and still healing may not come. There are things going on that we cannot see. We looked at Daniel in chapter 8. Daniel fasted and prayed for three weeks and still his prayer was not answered (Daniel 10:2). Finally, an angel came to explain that there were things going on in the spiritual realm that prevented the answer from coming (Daniel 10:13). Likewise, when we pray, the answer may not come, and we may not know the reason for a period or God may never reveal the reason to us.

Lutfor was diagnosed with spinal stenosis. Months earlier he had experienced a dramatic but temporary healing when a group of men prayed for him. Now, however, when he stands or walks for any length of time, pain develops in his lower left leg. One day, Lutfor and his colleagues came to our apartment to visit. Due to the lack of a hoped-for vehicle, he and his friends had walked five kilometers that day. Since he had been sitting in our house for about an hour, he wasn't feeling pain when I offered to pray for him. However, he expected his leg to bother him for the next several days.

It was late and I was tired. Still, I sensed that the Lord wanted him to be healed and wanted me to pray for him. I laid my right hand on his shoulder and prayed. As I prayed, I felt warmth on the top of my hand, not the part that was touching his body. This warmth is frequently a sign of the presence and power of God.

After my prayer, I asked Lutfor to stand and walk around the living room for a few minutes. It wasn't long before he began to feel pain in his leg. Even though I had responded to what I believed the Lord was telling me to do, and I was aware of the presence of the Holy Spirit and the power of God, Lutfor was not healed. There are times when, like Daniel, we simply do not know what is going on in the spiritual realm.[2]

Conclusion

In this chapter we looked at reasons why people do not experience the healing that God is willing to give. Understanding these reasons can help in diagnosis when people are not healed. They can help us on our path of learning, and help us not to get discouraged.

Key Bible Passage

In this passage we see the disciples searching for the reason behind a failed deliverance.

> A man in the crowd answered, "Teacher, I brought you my son, who is possessed by a spirit that has robbed him of speech. Whenever it seizes him, it throws him to the ground. He foams at the mouth, gnashes his teeth and becomes rigid. I asked your disciples to drive out the spirit, but they could not."...

---

2. There is a happy ending to this story. Sometime after I prayed for him, Lutfor applied for a passport so that he could travel to India for treatment for his back. While walking out of the passport office with his new passport, his back was healed. As of this writing, he is still healed, almost a year after collecting his passport. I make no claim that Lutfor was healed as a result of my ministry to him; I am just happy that he is pain free.

> After Jesus had gone indoors, his disciples asked him privately, "Why couldn't we drive it out?" (Mark 9:17–18, 28)

Teaser

In the conclusion, we will look at some ways to implement what we have learned.

Closing Prayer

Lord Jesus, help us not to give up when we don't see the results that we long to see. Help us to keep learning and growing. Help us to always go back to you so that we can process our failures with you.

Conclusion: Every Prayer Counts

Don't Give Up!

As we draw our journey to a close, I'll talk about the importance of persistence and the fears that block us. Finally, I'll end with some suggestions as to what you can do to begin practically implementing the concepts in this book. But first, a parable.

A Huge Pile of Sand and Gravel

A lone traveler was walking along a deserted path to his destination in the foothills of the Himalayas. On his left, the sheer rock face towered above him. To his right, the mountain dropped down into the gorge below. Despite the steepness of the mountain, the road was solid and the traveler's footing was sure. The sun was high, and our friend, the traveler, hoped to reach his destination before evening. As he rounded a bend in the path, he stopped short. His way was blocked by a pile of debris. The previous night, a mountain goat had dislodged a boulder higher on the cliff face. As the boulder crashed down the side of the mountain into the valley below, loose sand and gravel followed it, completely blocking the path.

Walking around the pile of debris was impossible. If he tried to do so, he would fall off the edge of the cliff. Climbing over the barrier was too dangerous. If the sand shifted, he would be swept off the mountain. His only option was to remove the debris handful by handful. He set his backpack down and removed his steel dinner plate. Then he got to work, scooping up the debris with his plate and dumping it over the edge. After the first hour of toil, it looked like his efforts were in vain. The pile of debris was still as imposing as ever. Our traveler, however, was not one to give up. Two hours later, he could see that he had made a little progress. Four hours later, there was hope that eventually his path would be clear. Just before dusk, he cleared the path and continued on his journey.

In my parable, the huge pile of sand and gravel is a friend's sickness. Each handful of debris represents the effect of one prayer. Every prayer counts even though we often cannot see any change. Unfortunately, we usually give up before the debris is gone.

The Unjust Judge

Jesus taught his disciples to be persistent. He described a widow facing an intransigent and unjust judge. The widow kept coming to him with her plea. Eventually the judge dealt with her case simply to get her off his case (Luke 18:1–8). We read this story and mistakenly assume that God is the unjust judge in the parable, reluctant and unwilling to answer our prayers. But, we think, if we just pester him enough, maybe he will relent and grant our request. That, however, is an incorrect view of our heavenly Father. God is not the unjust judge in the parable, the problem we face is. Just as every petition wore the judge down, so every prayer wears down the problem we face.

We find persistence in prayer difficult because we cannot see the effect of our prayers. *What effect does my prayer have upon such a severe sickness?* we think. So, in discouragement, we give up before the task is done.

Every faith-filled prayer has effect. When the disciples came to Jesus and asked him to increase their faith, he responded, "If you have faith as small as a mustard seed, you can say to this mulberry tree, 'Be uprooted and planted in the sea,' and it will obey you" (Luke 17:6). Jesus was telling them not to focus on the size of their faith. Rather, he was telling them to use the faith they had, no matter how small.

Faith that is very small, particularly when consistently applied, can work powerful effects.

Facing Our Fears

Now we know how to heal the sick in Jesus' name, but still we hesitate. We are held back by fear. What if we pray for someone and they are not healed? Won't this destroy their faith? On the face of it, this reasoning appears valid. We don't want to be the one who causes a person to turn away from the Lord in disappointment. On a deeper level, we worry that if we pray in Jesus' name and the person is not healed, then we will bring dishonor to the name of Jesus. Isn't protecting God's honor a good thing? Let's look at one man who tried to protect God's honor and ended up displeasing God in the process.

Uzzah and the Ark of God

In 1 Chronicles 13, we read how King David, along with the whole assembly of Israel, decided to bring the ark to where he lived, Jerusalem. Contrary to the Old Testament instructions on how the ark is to be handled, David and his men chose to transport the ark on an oxcart.

Uzzah was guiding the ark, but despite his best efforts, the oxen stumbled. Uzzah reached out his hand to steady the ark (1 Chronicles 13:7–10). It appears that Uzzah's intentions were good. The ark, standing over two feet tall, with the wings of cherubim covering the top, and overlaid in solid gold, would have been a wondrous sight. If the precious ark were to fall off the cart and break, it would be a catastrophe, bringing shame to the name of the Lord. Uzzah, not wanting

God's honor to be damaged, did the thing he thought best—he reached out to steady the ark. God struck him dead.

If we probe a little deeper, however, we may discover that Uzzah was concerned about something else in addition to God's honor. As the one guiding the oxen, if something were to happen, he would be the responsible party. His honor would be damaged as well.

We make a grave error when we take on the burden of upholding the glory of the Lord. Uzzah would have known what happened to the ark after it was captured by the Philistines during the time of Eli. The Philistine leaders placed the ark in front of the idol of Dagon, their god. The next morning, Dagon was lying prostrate before the ark (1 Samuel 5:1–4). God is able to uphold his own honor.

By hesitating to pray for someone out of fear that God's honor will come crashing to the ground like the ark falling off the oxcart, aren't we being a little like Uzzah? God is more than capable of upholding his own honor. Our duty is not to uphold God's honor. Our duty is to obey.

But What If I Destroy Someone's Faith?

Sometimes we are afraid to pray because we are afraid that if the person is not healed then it will cause them to turn away from the Lord. Won't a failed healing cause a person to abandon their faith? The reality is that most people don't expect much anyway. Most have never seen an instant healing in response to prayer, much less experienced one in their own bodies. If they are not healed, there is no great letdown to their faith.

No New Blood Cells

Gabriella woke up on May 14, 2021, and then fainted. A 911 call led to a ten-day stay in the hospital. Doctors said that she had a very low blood count and that her bone marrow was no longer producing new blood cells. She had been home for a couple of days when I phoned her. We talked for a while, and I prayed for her over the phone. As far as I could tell, there was absolutely no change in her medical condition as a result of my prayer.

Rather than losing faith in God, Gabriella said to me, "It was really sweet of you to reach out and pray for me in this way." At the end of the prayer time, she told me that her heart was softer toward God because of the prayer time. Gabriella was not harmed by my "failure," rather, she was encouraged spiritually.[1]

The fear that no results from our prayers will cause a person to lose their faith in God or will lead to God's glory being tarnished, can be a tool of the Enemy to stop us from reaching out in care and compassion to those who are sick. The danger comes when we promise healing. Promising something that God has not told us to promise can cause people to lose their faith in God.

Practical Action Steps

We have now come to the end of our journey. How can the teaching in this book become part of your life? How can you become an agent of healing? In the section below, I present several action steps.

Look for Opportunities to Practice

Like any other spiritual task, ministering healing to others effectively takes training. If you want to grow in ministering healing to others, then look for opportunities to practice. If you notice that a friend has a cold, ask if you can pray for them. If you want to take the pressure off, you could say, "Hey, I'm learning how to pray for the sick. Do you mind if I practice on you?" Most people will be happy to be a subject of your practice. If you still don't get

---

1. Two years later, one Sunday after I preached at their church, Gabriella's parents came up to me and thanked me for praying for their daughter. She had had a bone marrow transplant and was now living a normal, healthy life.

enough opportunities to practice, you could pray daily that God will give you opportunities to minister healing to people.

Focus on Obedience, Not Results

If we constantly focus on results, then we will quickly become frustrated. Rather than focus on results, focus on being obedient to Jesus. Simply offering to pray for someone is a step of obedience. After one of my early prayer times, I told God, *Lord, I think I did what you wanted me to do. The results are in your hands.* Later, I heard that the man I'd prayed for experienced healing.

Practice Commanding

For some people, it is hard to say, "I command the pain to go away" or "I command this knee to be healed in Jesus' name." We just aren't used to speaking to body parts and it may feel awkward at first. Yet, speaking with authority in this way is foundational to ministering healing. After you issue a command, check with the patient to see how they are feeling. Sometimes the effects of the command are slightly delayed. If there is no immediate improvement, you can check again in fifteen minutes.

If you feel self-conscious issuing commands to backs and knees or telling diseases to depart, there is one thing you can do to get over your awkwardness. You can practice on yourself. That brings us to our next suggestion.

Practice on Yourself

There is no prohibition in the Bible against ministering healing to yourself. The great thing about practicing on yourself is that you don't have to worry about what the patient is going to think about you. You can also take as long as you want without wondering if the patient is starting to feel uncomfortable. The next time you have a headache, rather than immediately reaching for the Tylenol, you could take five minutes to rebuke the pain in Jesus' name. Then check in with yourself ten minutes later to see how you feel. This brings us to the next point.

Take Before-and-After Measurements

If you want to know if healing has started to occur, then you need to know how bad the problem was before you started to minister. You can ask questions like, "How bad is that headache on a scale of one to ten?" Or, "How far can you bend that sore knee?" Then after ministering, ask again. "You could only bend it thirty degrees before we prayed—how far can you bend it now?"

Before-and-after measurements are often subjective. Indeed, the experience of pain itself is subjective and difficult to accurately quantify. Yet asking before-and-after questions primes both the patient and the one ministering healing to expect change. This kind of question raises faith because it creates an expectation that something will happen during the prayer time.

Keep a Prayer Record

Julius Caesar said, "Experience is the teacher of all things,"[2] or, as it is more commonly put, "Experience is the best teacher." It is, however, more accurate to say, "Reflected experience is the best teacher."[3] Each prayer time is an opportunity to reflect and learn. Was the patient fully healed? Partially? What made it easy to pray this time? What made it difficult? How could the prayer time be handled differently if there were an opportunity to do it over? How did you feel about the ministry time? Do you believe you did what the Lord was asking you to do?

---

2. Flexner, *Wise Words and Wives' Tales*, 55.

3. I got this from Sherwood Lingenfelter, author of *Leadership in the Way of the Cross: Forging Ministry from the Crucible of Crisis*, Wipf & Stock (2018), during a teaching session in Torre Pellice, Italy, in September 2019.

I suggest making notes on all the people you pray for. In my own record, I note the date, the patient's name and symptoms, and then I write a short paragraph describing what happened. If on a subsequent date I get an update, I later add that to my record as well.

The point of taking notes is to provide an opportunity for reflection and learning on what went well, what did not, and how one could do better in the future.

Practice in Community

Sometimes we are scared when we are alone, but more willing to take risks when someone else is with us. Faith increases when you pray with a like-minded person. In addition, praying with another person allows us to compare notes with others on how they experienced the prayer time.

Recently, Ingrid invited me to pray for one of her stroke patients. As I was praying, Ingrid noticed that an adult nephew of the patient who'd joined us in the room had tears in his eyes. It seems that the Lord touched him in some way while we prayed for his aunt. I would never have realized this if I had been ministering alone.

Ministering with another person allows time for debriefing. Once while my friend Jonathan and I were chatting with a group of guys, I received the distinct impression that the person sitting on my left was struggling with a particular sin. I didn't confront the person and afterward I wondered if I was totally off base. On the way home, I debriefed with Jonathan and he confirmed my impression. Similarly, when we minister healing with another person, we can compare notes later.

Keep Learning

One way to learn is to process your prayer times with Jesus. Using your prayer record as a starting point, talk to Jesus about how you ministered. Ask him if he has any instruction for you or any suggestions for how to minister differently in the future.

Resources can also assist in our learning. There are numerous books on healing. There are also many online courses available. Some resources that have been helpful for me are listed in the bibliography. If you have the opportunity to learn together in a group, even better. If you are part of a home group, you could read through a book on healing during your weekly meetings and then discuss the content together. If the group is open to the idea, you could use part of your group time each week to pray for any sicknesses in the group.

Conclusion

May you step out with courage and obedience to minister healing to the sick. May you become an agent of healing.

Key Bible Passage

> Heal the sick, raise the dead, cleanse those who have leprosy, drive out demons. Freely you have received; freely give. (Matthew 10:8)

Closing Prayer

Lord Jesus, help us to go out and do what you commanded us to do. Help us to do what you did. Help us to heal the sick in your name.

To ask questions, provide feedback, or enquire about speaking events and training programs offered, write to us at info@swordfish-publishing.com or visit the Contact Us page of https://swordfish-publishing.com/

Acknowledgments

I have drawn from many different sources for this book. Some of them have become part of who I am and so it is virtually impossible to identify them all, much less give them credit. But there are a few that I would like to specially mention. I have watched several teaching sessions by Art Thomas on YouTube and have absorbed many of his ideas, particularly earlier on in my journey of learning to minister healing. Curry Blake has an extensive teaching on healing available called "Divine Healing Technician." I have learned a lot from him, especially that people don't have to get cleaned up spiritually before they receive healing. Dr. Roger Sapp's "Christ Centered Healing Seminar" (also available on YouTube) is helpful as well.

The books I have drawn from are listed in the notes. However, I want to draw special attention to Jordan Seng's *Miracle Work*. I have cited his book several times. He added much clarity to ideas that were already circulating in my brain at the time of writing.

Personally, I want to especially thank Beth Brown and Jonathan Ammon. They were the first to read an earlier edition of this book and provided super-encouraging feedback. Rev. Paul Woodburn and Clinton Moore provided many excellent comments and, in some places, helpful challenges to my ideas and some of the ways I stated those ideas. Their feedback has made this book a much better product and I have adopted many of their suggestions, though I take final responsibility for the way things are stated.

Working with editor Jessica Snell has been a real joy. I am highly impressed by her sharp eye and dedication to making this project as good as it can be.

Now a word to my father: Dad, I remember that time in Tsavo National Park in Kenya when we still lived in Africa. Our car broke down and we were stranded. We were not looking forward to spending a night on that very untraveled road in the company of whatever lions and hyenas happened to be prowling around the area. Eventually, our car, with all of us still inside, was towed to our lodging area. There, still in the middle of the game park, and far from medical attention, I came down with a fever. I remember you praying for me that night. As you prayed for me, you no doubt remembered the time I came down with cerebral malaria some fourteen years earlier while I was a baby in Somalia. I would perhaps have died as an infant, had it not been for the doctors who just happened to be nearby, attending a retirement party for one of their colleagues. You have prayed for me daily for most of my life and continue to do so. As I have gotten older, I have had a few opportunities to pray for you as well. Thank you, Dad.

Finally, I want to express my appreciation to Ingrid for our last nineteen years together. Thanks, Ingrid, for being a great friend and partner in ministry. And for finding people for me to pray for.

Bibliography

Allen, David, OSB. "Christian Asceticism," *Obsculta* 15, issue 1 (2022): 52–60. https://digitalcommons.csbsju.edu/obsculta/vol15/iss1/7.

Biasi, Fiorella, Monica Deiana, Tina Guina, Paola Gamba, Gabriella Leonarduzzi, and Giuseppe Poli. "Wine Consumption and Intestinal Redox Homeostasis." National Library of Medicine, June 18, 2024. https://www.ncbi.nlm.nih.gov/pmc/articles/PMC4085343/.

Blue, Ken. *Authority to Heal*. Downers Grove, Illinois: InterVarsity Press, 1987. Kindle.

Bradley, David. "Why Gladwell's 10,000-hour Rule Is Wrong." BBC, November 13, 2012. https://www.bbc.com/future/article/20121114-gladwells-10000-hour-rule-myth.

Busenitz, Nathan. "The Personal Reformation of Martin Luther." *The Master's Seminary Blog*, October 25, 2016. https://blog.tms.edu/the-personal-reformation-of-martin-luther.

De Arteaga, William L. *Agnes Sanford and Her Companions: The Assault on Cessationism and the Coming of the Charismatic Renewal*. Eugene, Oregon: Wipf & Stock, 2015.

Encyclopedia.com. "Hindu and Buddhist Asceticism." Accessed December 31, 2023. https://www.encyclopedia.com/history/dictionaries-thesauruses-pictures-and-press-releases/hindu-and-buddhist-asceticism.

Flexner, Stuart Berg. *Wise Words and Wives' Tales: The Origins, Meanings and Time-honored Wisdom of Proverbs and Folk Sayings, Olde and New*. New York: Avon Books, 1993.

Gilger, Mark. "MC Man Charged with Resisting Arrest and Possessing Drugs, Knife and Incapacitation Device." *The Standard-Journal*, September 9, 2021. https://www.standard-journal.com/article_e7d570a3-56de-5bab-b85d-c653fb41909e.html.

Gladwell, Malcolm. *Outliers: The Story of Success*. New York: Little, Brown and Company, 2008.

Got Questions Ministries. "What Does 2 Corinthians 12:7 Mean?" Accessed December 31, 2023. https://www.bibleref.com/2-Corinthians/12/2-Corinthians-12-7.html.

Guretzki, David. "Not Everything Has a Purpose." *Faith Today*, October 7, 2021. https://www.faithtoday.ca/Magazines/2021-Sept-Oct/Not-everything-has-a-purpose.

Harrell, David Edwin. *All Things Are Possible: The Healing and Charismatic Revivals in Modern America*. First Indiana University Press paperback edition. Bloomington: Indiana University Press, 1978. Kindle.

Horrobin, Peter. *Healing through Deliverance*. Lancaster, England: Sovereign World Ltd, 2008. Kindle.

Keener, Craig S., *Miracles*. 2 vols. Grand Rapids, Michigan: Baker Academic, 2011.

Keener, Craig S. *Miracles Today*. Grand Rapids, Michigan: Baker Academic, 2021.

Lake, John G. *Adventures in God*. Tulsa, OK: Harrison House, 1981.

Liddell, Henry George, and Robert Scott. *A Greek-English Lexicon*, revised and augmented throughout by Sir Henry Stuart Jones, with the assistance of Roderick McKenzie. Oxford: Clarendon Press, 1940. https://www.perseus.tufts.edu/hopper/text?doc=Perseus%3Atext%3A1999.04.0057%3Aentry%3Ddu%2Fnamis.

Mickelson's Enhanced Strong's Dictionaries of the Greek and Hebrew Testaments, 2nd ed. Kennesaw, Georgia: LivingSon, 2015.

Nee, Watchman. *The Latent Power of the Soul.* New York: Christian Fellowship Publishers, Inc., 1972.

Ohnishi, S. Tsuyoshi, "Ki: A Key to Transform the Century of Death to the Century of Life." National Library of Medicine, March 12, 2007. https://www.ncbi.nlm.nih.gov/pmc/articles/PMC1978229/.

Oxford Languages, Oxford University Press. Definition of "agent." Accessed November 30, 2023, via Google search (see explanation here for context: https://languages.oup.com/google-dictionary-en/).

Roberts, Oral. *The Call.* Garden City, New York: Doubleday & Company, Inc., 1972.

Seng, Jordan. *Miracle Work: A Down-to-Earth Guide to Supernatural Ministries.* Downers Grove, Illinois: InterVarsity Press, 2013. Kindle.

Sproul, R. C. "Discerning God's Will: The Three Wills of God." Monergism.com, Adapted from an August 1993 article in Ligonier Ministries' *Tabletalk* magazine. Accessed December 31, 2023. https://www.monergism.com/discerning-god%E2%80%99s-will-three-wills-god.

Thomas, Art, and James Loruss. Produced by Art Thomas. *Paid in Full.* Supernatural Truth Productions, August 18, 2014. Manwaring quotation starts at 1:12:30. https://vimeo.com/ondemand/paidinfull.

Valantasis, Richard. "Constructions of Power in Asceticism." *Journal of the American Academy of Religion* 63, no. 4 (Winter 2015): 775–821. https://www.jstor.org/stable/1465468.

Viola, Frank. "Rethinking Paul's Thorn in the Flesh." *Beyond Evangelical: The Blog of Frank Viola,* April 24, 2012. https://www.frankviola.org/2012/04/24/paulsthornintheflesh/.

Weisse, M. E., B. Eberly, and D. A. Person, "Wine as a Digestive Aid: Comparative Antimicrobial Effects of Bismuth Salicylate and Red and White Wine." National Library of Medicine, December 23, 1995. https://www.ncbi.nlm.nih.gov/pmc/articles/PMC2539099/.

Wigglesworth, Smith. *Ever Increasing Faith.* Springfield, Missouri: Gospel Publishing House, 1972.

Wikipedia. "Christian Views on the Old Covenant." Accessed December 31, 2023. https://en.wikipedia.org/wiki/Christian_views_on_the_Old_Covenant.

Wikipedia.org. "Qi." Accessed December 21, 2023. https://en.wikipedia.org/wiki/Qi.

Wikipedia. "Self-flagellation." Accessed December 31, 2023. https://en.wikipedia.org/wiki/Self-flagellation.

Willard, Dallas. *The Divine Conspiracy: Rediscovering Our Hidden Life in God*. San Francisco: HarperOne, 1998.

Willard, Dallas. *The Spirit of the Disciplines: Understanding How God Changes Lives*. San Francisco: HarperOne, 1999.

Wommack, Andrew. "You've Already Got It," Lesson 6, "The Problem Is Our Unbelief." The referenced incident starts at minute 30. Andrew Wommack Ministries (website). https://www.awmi.net/audio/audio-teachings/?teaching=youve-already-got-it&lesson=the-problem-is-our-unbelief.

World Population Review. "How Many People Die Each Day in 2024?" Accessed November 28, 2023. https://worldpopulationreview.com/countries/deaths-per-day.

www.ingramcontent.com/pod-product-compliance
Lightning Source LLC
Chambersburg PA
CBHW072157070526
44585CB00015B/1186